Adaptation to Climate Change

Adaptation to Climate Change

Authors

Austin Mardon

Faith Grace Robes

Hafsa Binte Younus

Hannah Nie

Jannat Irfan

Mahnoor Irfan

Rawan Ahmed

Razan Ahmed

Simon Garneau

Syed Rizvi

Zarmminaa Rehman

Edited By

Erwin Kwok

First Printing: 2023

Typeset and Cover Design by Josh Harnack

ISBN: 978-1-77369-899-1
eBook ISBN: 978-1-77369-902-8

Golden Meteorite Press
103 11919 82 St NW
Edmonton, AB T5B 2W3
www.goldenmeteoritepress.com

Table of Contents

Introduction

As pollutant emissions continue being released, deleterious consequences are inevitable for human livelihood. However, the situation is not entirely somber and grim. Some developments have taken place through both technological advances and scientific research.

In this book, we take an in-depth look at anthropogenic adaptations to climate change which may curtail or impede the impacts of climate change. The following 10 chapters focus on the themes of food security, energy production, and livelihood changes that affect areas such as housing and employment opportunities.

Join us as we wade through the intricacies of anthropogenic climate adaptations to understand how the repercussions of industrial capitalism can be mitigated.

Chapter 1
Housing Adaptation

Simon Garneau

Introduction

With changing climates, cultures, and economies, this instability presents housing as an increasingly difficult issue to address. As populations are growing, the need to meet housing demands grows as well. Increasingly in the media, the younger generations are told that houses are scarce and the financial requirements are seemingly always reaching new levels of impossibility. Around the world, more and more areas are affected by natural disasters wiping areas clean of any habitable homes. Tearing down years of work and time invested in a single day. Those who are lucky to remain untouched by the devastation of nature are susceptible to other complications. Such as older people are living on average longer lives and find themselves, depending on cultures and family dynamics, spending their remaining time left, alone and isolated. These issues, challenges, and unfortunate realities need to be tackled through a durable and sustainable housing initiative. Adapting and dealing with these issues opens the way for the innovative use of new carbon-free technologies as well as durable and recyclable methods. These houses and housing buildings or units need to adapt and account for the multiple challenges of the present, today. Challenges such as proximity to public transit, the establishment of community, and greener surroundings, all need to have a positive impact on the environment and if possible, as well a smaller reliance on polluting materials. Thankfully, housing development companies and researchers are constantly figuring out how to tackle these challenges and as a result, churn out a large diversity of different sustainable, environment-positive ways, adaptative and potential solutions, to shelter different communities.

Research

The large number of research used throughout this chapter comes from the Canadian government, Canadian companies and academic research papers related to housing in Canada found on the information database Clarivate. Other countries have paged the way for innovation and have come across significant challenges throughout their development. Therefore, they provide us with great resources, convenient innovations, and concepts that will be taken and used in this chapter. The main example is the Passive House Institute in Germany which provides guidelines and certifications that are used within Canada. Given that Canada has a unique landscape, climate, and set of resources when compared to most countries the focus remains largely here. Research on Canadian data and techniques of adaptation that take into account all of these factors, facilitates the research aspect and allows the reader to keep the same and possibly familiar frame of reference.

Housing in Canada

Grasping and obtaining a clear understanding of every single housing market and set of criteria can also become overwhelming and complicates the comparisons. The way we are defining housing groups in this chapter will largely rely on information directly taken from statistics Canada. Housing in Canada is separated into 5 groups by Statistics Canada; single detached houses, apartments in a building that has five or more storeys, apartments in a building that has fewer than five storeys, apartments or flats in a duplex, and other dwellings. The most popular being "Single-detached houses represented 53.6% of all dwelling types in 2016" (Census in Brief: Dwellings in Canada, Census year 2016, 2017). Canada is also the 2nd largest country in the world and has a population density of 3.9 people per square kilometer, Canadian cities are less densely populated than many of their counterparts in Europe and the United States (Canadian Population, 2022). This information provides a clear conceptualisation and model for the current housing set up in Canada. Demonstrating that housing is separated and more spaced out compared to European cities, which have been around for centuries and have adapted throughout history to meet the population's housing needs.

Green house gas emissions (GHG)

GHGs reduction in the development of new dwellings is important to tackle climate change. The housing industry contributes a large amount of GHG into the atmosphere. Therefore, the first factor we are looking to address in housing is the reduction of the GHGs emitted during the lifecycle of a dwelling. There is lots of room for improvement when it comes to greenhouse gas reduction in the building sector, a study done in 2021 by Li et al., compiled data and found that "GHG emissions from new single-detached households can be reduced up to 77% and 89%, respectively if the most stringent level (i.e., Step 5) of BC Step Code or the Passive House criteria is implemented nationwide." (Li et al., 2021). Passive housing is defined, to the standards of Passive House Institute, as dwellings with a "high level of thermal comfort with minimum energy consumption" (Criteria for the Passive House, EnerPHit and PHI Low Energy Building Standard Structure criteria, 2015), the passive housing standard refers to new developments, as older buildings most often cannot reach the criteria due to the substantial improvements and resources needed to meet the standards. With the rising need for housing in Canada, new dwellings will be the main focus of the GHG emission reduction paragraph. First, we will analyze the programs used in Canada to reduce energy consumption. Then we analyze a housing development company that takes action in lowering its environmental impact. Continuing on the GHGs reduction topic we will take on a different perspective and try to predict ways that housing might change and adapt to the effects of climate change.

Energy efficient programs

To get a simple idea of what an energy-efficient program looks like, we will more closely examine the two examples below that are used to build energy-efficient housing and buildings in Canada. These programs all have as a goal to reduce carbon emissions and GHGs emissions. The first program is the Passive House institute, which is recognized globally when it comes to building energy-efficient products. In North America, the organization that certifies buildings meet its standards is called The North American Certifiers Circle ("NACC"). Its criteria are based on low maximum space cooling and heating, air tightness, and primary energy demand. Another program that is used in Canada is the Net Zero Home Labelling Program ("CHBA"). With over 1000 homes labelled, the CHBA defines "net zero homes" as homes that produce as much clean energy as they consume annually, using on-site renewable energy systems." (CHBA). The differences between the two-labeling program are that the Passive House Institute (PHI) focuses on reducing energy consumption and keeping it low. Comparatively, the Net Zero Home (CHBA) program is not primarily engineered to reduce energy consumption but to ensure they only consume as much as they produce. For instance, a sustainability article published in 2019 found that the extra cost and "lack of knowledge about the technology associated with a net zero energy home" (Singh et al., 2019) were not the reason behind the lack of homeowners of net zero homes. Instead, it came from construction and design quality. Meaning the lack of development in net zero homes comes from the home builders' skepticism towards the potential demand for that market, as well as the ability to make trade-offs that would not affect the quality of the home.

Development companies

Understanding how housing development companies take action in reducing their GHGs emissions is necessary, it allows those outside this domain to understand the steps taken to tackle ongoing environmental challenges. Our first case study is a real estate company that builds and rents out housing in Canada and the U.S. This analysis of a more environmentally conscious housing development business model is based on their sustainability report. We can observe how they adapted to building more efficiently throughout the years. The actions this company takes to reduce its carbon footprint and reduce its environmental impact are numerous and a first step towards reducing GHG in the housing development processes. They tracked that 80% of construction waste was diverted from landfills. This is great when it comes to reducing the impact of housing construction which can be a large issue since construction waste is hard to recycle and often ends up filling landfills. Their normalized leaking rate used to track air tightness was around 0.14 (p 40) which is an improvement from when they first started to track this data. Having less air leakage prevents loss of heat in a home, the more efficiently a house can retain this heat the less energy it needs to use to maintain the internal temperature of the home. They informed themselves with the Net zero home labeling program. (Minto, 2021).

Changing needs and housing adaptation

What are the solutions to improve housing adaptabilities when it comes to older occupants and reduces the GHGs emitted per household? As Canada's population is aging, we can observe that 18.8% of the population is at least 65 years of age, and children aged 0 to 14 represent 15.6% of the population (StatCan, 2022). The higher level of older people will bring about a need to change housing, considering also the fact that as less housing becomes available more people will resort to living with their aging parents (StatCan, 2022). This can result in split housing models. Future damages and health challenges might also become more frequent and cause an increase in people with disabilities (WHO, 2022). The proximity of young and old generations creates a mutualistic socioeconomic relationship, leading to an indirect way of reducing the GHGs and potential waste created, as we focus on building communities. One way to create these communities and bring about the necessary adaption to the changing housing landscape is through the retrofitting of houses to fit more people (Prevost, 2015). The popular housing model in Canada consists of houses in a suburban neighbourhood, meaning a small number of people occupy those large areas. To navigate these neighbourhoods and access other amenities, those residents highly rely on cars as a means of transport. With the rising cost of living, fewer and fewer people will be able to afford those large suburban houses, coupled with the necessary transport vehicle. With an increase in population density within these neighbourhoods, walkable neighbourhoods are more likely to emerge.

Walkable neighbourhoods have been found to bring about more social capital to the individuals living there meaning that people are more socially engaged with their communities and more trusting as a result of walkable neighbourhoods (Leyden, 2003). With a stronger community sense, we get the early development of a circular economy (Yu, 2007) as people are more inclined to trade between each other instead of selling outside the community bubble. Walkable neighbourhoods also justify a lesser reliance on cars, as they are not needed as much compared to other neighbourhood models, to participate in social activities. Whereas in car-centric neighbourhoods to get to any location to socialize there usually is a driving distance to be made. In addition, the clustering of a larger number of people in a smaller space allows for an increase in access to the efficient use of civil infrastructure (Blais, 2011) as well as reducing the potential expansion in the future, needed to cater to those outside the service area. The resulting changes affecting people's living conditions from climate change are likely to push people closer together, as houses and homes are subject to destruction from more frequent natural disasters and the loss of wealth through economic struggle requires the rise of more and more communal living settings.

Adaptation to natural disasters

An aspect to consider with housing adaptation is the issue of vulnerability, as climate change can bring about more recurrent ecological disasters. The geological topography of a region is an important factor and dictates how likely the disaster is to occur, and the magnitude of the damages. When it comes to flooding is the most frequent natural disaster in Canada (Gov Canada, 2022) there are several ways to ensure the house someone lives in can withstand flooding. One of them is to have airtight windows, this gives a protection barrier against water coming in. Airtight windows are also coincidentally a common criterion for efficient energy use, therefore proving useful in more than one way, although this specification is not mentioned in the documents and should not be assumed to be entirely flood resistant. For smaller floods and ground-level windows, installing flood barriers can protect the basement of a home. When building new houses in flood prominent areas, elevation, floodwalls, dry/wet floodproofing and floating homes are all methods of adapting to the potential occurrence of flooding.

Measures to protect dwellings from natural disasters are limited and rely on protection from outside the house. Communities are better off investing in ways to protect their homes communally instead of having each house take action independently, free of communication. This ensures that those lacking in funds or proper response time can be effectively protected from the damages of natural disasters, as well as making communities aware of those more susceptible to damages. However, the more measures that are set in place the greater the chances of a home surviving a natural disaster, this leads to fewer damages. Overall, these protection measures reduce the possible pollution and emissions that would have resulted from the disaster, allowing houses to be kept in use for longer and requiring no new developments to be built. Hopefully, the houses that are still standing improve in methods of protection against natural disasters, keeping those communities alive, safe, and adapting.

Housing longevity

Earlier, we mentioned the concept of circular economy, which refers to the reuse of products to elongate their lifecycle. This was discussed after the section on the emissions of GHGs in buildings that utilise energy-efficient methods of conservation on an operational timeline. This paragraph will focus on the preservation and elongation of a building's lifetime. For a building to be efficient throughout its life and to compensate for any pollution, emission, or any other environmental impact it needs to have a long life of use (Tarpio, 2020). Through a circular economy, the use of a building can be extended, and stay in the housing market for as long as possible which is an important factor to consider when building (Stahel, 1981). Renovations are costly and the layout of a house can determine whether or not it is fit for living. Those changes are bound to arise as families and people living together experience changes in economic standing, environmental perspectives, and the number of children they have. These changes may be affected by cultural shifts as well with immigration being much more common as international communities develop in different areas of the country. When building efficient energy housing those potential changes are an important factor to consider since the difference in demand can render the efficient houses useless and limit their lifetime.

One prominent example is by designing suburbs to "accommodate a blossoming market of new families, with father off to the office and mother at home looking after the children" (Nichols, 2013), those types of houses are still present today but less desirable. Families are often smaller than they use to be, roads are more congested and gas prices are higher, making the use of cars less efficient and no longer sought after. Much of the design for these neighborhoods relied on the unchanging family structure, consumer preferences when it comes to transport, and people's general enthusiasm towards driving. Now the situation has changed and the long commute is dreaded and can even potentially worsen people's mental state. This as been observed in a study where, there was a positive response when people switched over to public transport (Jacob, 2020), indicating that individuals are somewhat affected by their transportation methods. Several housing designs and different types of land plot utilization aim to fix this inflexible design flaw, hoping to achieve a more flexible type of housing to better accommodate the changing needs of individuals and families through time (MacBurnie, 2006). The longevity of a house and its ability to adapt through time, based on the homeowner's needs facilitates a stronger community, as we saw before, as people are more likely to stay and build strong bonds with those around them.

Overview and further links to climate change adaptations

Over the years multiple models of housing have been suggested, researched, and adopted, some concepts such as flexible housing, which have been present since the 1970s but haven't been fully embraced. Change takes time, and the most popular and effective adaptable housing in response to climate change at the moment is the improvement of a house's ability to rely on a lower supply of energy. Programs such as passive housing are a great way to determine how effective a house is on the international market when it comes to being energy efficient. Energy efficiency is also a great way of adapting to climate change as houses provide homeowners with greater cooling and heating differences, in the future as temperatures become often unpredictable, having the ability to rely less on energy, will mean that control of the home's temperature will not depend on economic well being. Energy-efficient housing, split housing model, communal living, flexible housing, and housing adaptations to natural disasters are all adapting in some shape or form to the challenges brought on by climate change. These solutions reduce the overall green house gas emissions coming from the housing sector and can reduce the emissions in adjacent sectors and industries.

Multiple reductions in different sectors can occur through the changing needs of people living in proximity to food, public transport, and social communities providing them with a network of trade and exchange reducing the need for exported goods. Given that energy efficiency reaches a level of positive or neutral impacts on the environment with this form of housing, compared to older models, which do not rely on new materials or new construction. Housing adaptation provides the world with a solution to reducing our impact and living more comfortably in the ever-changing world of today.

References

Abadie, A., & Imbens, G. W. (2011). Bias-corrected matching estimators for average treatment effects. Journal of Business and Economic Statistics, 29(1), 1–11. doi: 10.1198/JBES.2009.07333

Blais, P. (2011). Perverse cities: Hidden subsidies, wonky policy, and urban sprawl, UBC Press, Vancouver, BC.

Building Certification – Passive House Canada | Maison Passive Canada. (n.d.). Retrieved from https://www.passivehousecanada.com/passive-house-building-certification/

Census in Brief: Dwellings in Canada, Census year 2016. (n.d.). Retrieved from https://www12.statcan.gc.ca/census-recensement/2016/as-sa/98-200-x/2016005/98-200-x2016005-eng.cfm

Criteria for the Passive House, EnerPHit, and PHI Low Energy Building Standard Structure of the criteria. (2015). www.passivehouse.com

Disability. (n.d.). Retrieved from https://www.who.int/news-room/fact-sheets/detail/disability-and-health

Prevost, G., Baetz, B. W., Asce, M., Razavi, S., & El-Dakhakhni, W. (2014). Retrofitting Suburban Homes for Resiliency: Design Principles. Journal of Urban Planning and Development, 141(3), 04014027. doi: 10.1061/(ASCE)UP.1943-5444.0000217

Femenias, P., & Geromel, F. (2020). Adaptable housing? A quantitative study of contemporary apartment layouts that have been rearranged by end-users. Journal of Housing and the Built Environment, 35, 481–505. doi: 10.1007/s10901-019-09693-9

Guidelines Guidelines for the Administration of Variances for Zero Emission Buildings in RS, RT, and RA Districts. (n.d.).

Jacob, N., Munford, L., Rice, N., & Roberts, J. (2021). Does commuting mode choice impact health? Health Economics (United Kingdom), 30(2), 207–230. doi: 10.1002/HEC.4184

NZE Program Landing Page - Net Zero Program Official Launch. (n.d.). Retrieved from https://www.chba.ca/CHBA/HousingCanada/Net_Zero_Energy_Program/CHBA/Housing_in_Canada/Net_Zero_Energy_Program/NZE_Program_Landing_Page.aspx

Leyden, K. (2003). "Social capital and the built environment: The importance of walkable neighborhoods." J. Public Health, 93(9), 1546–1551.

Li, B., Rowe, A., & Wild, P. (2021). Energy code effectiveness on GHG emission mitigation for single-family houses in Canada. doi: 10.1016/j.jclepro.2021.126840

Röck, M., Saade, M. R. M., Balouktsi, M., Rasmussen, F. N., Birgisdottir, H., Frischknecht, R., Habert, G., Lützkendorf, T., & Passer, A. (2020). Embodied GHG emissions of buildings – the hidden challenge for effective climate change mitigation. Applied Energy, 258(1), 107-114.

Stahel, W., & Reday-Mulvey, G. (1981). Jobs for tomorrow. The potential for substituting manpower for energy. Vantage Press.

Singh, R., Walsh, P., & Mazza, C. (n.d.). Sustainable Housing: Understanding the Barriers to Adopting Net Zero Energy Homes in Ontario, Canada. doi: 10.3390/su11226236

Chapter 2

Preservation and Restoration of Peatlands

Faith Grace Robes

Introduction

Canada is home to a third of the world's natural carbon storage, peatlands. Peatlands are a form of wetlands that have peat at the surface of the land. They store twice as much carbon as the entire forest biomass across the world, despite covering only 3% of the land (Humpenöder et al., 2020). The majority of peatlands are found in Asia (38.4%) and North America, mostly in Canada and Alaska (31.6%) (Xu et al., 2018). Followed by Europe (12.5%), South America (11.5%), Africa (4.4%), and Australia and Oceania (1.6%) (Joosten & Clarke, 2002; IPS, 2020). The waterlogged conditions, insufficient oxygen, high acidity, and nutrient deficiency prevents plants from completely decomposing, and through time, the partially decayed material forms peat soil. In the Northern Hemisphere, peatlands are found to be mosses, sedges, and shrubs. While in the topics, peatlands are naturally forested (UK Centre for Ecology & Hydrology, n.d.). Over thousands of years, thick layers of carbon-rich peat accumulated over these lands, thus, creating a disproportionately larger ratio of carbon than ecosystems on mineral soil (Joosten, 2015). This large carbon storage absorbs the carbon from the atmosphere providing a net-cooling effect to help mitigate the severe climate crisis (ICUN, 2022). Due to its carbon-rich ecosystem, peatlands have a water table close to the surface and its mosses. Having a water table close to the surface allows for anoxic decomposition, a condition wherein oxygen is not present but nitrates are involved. The importance of anoxic decomposition is that it reduces carbon losses from the system. The mosses further slow the decomposition rates by forming a recalcitrant litter. Peatlands also support a special fire-resistant moss known as sphagnum. This moss acts as a fire break to prevent any wild fires from spreading and limit the amount of carbon emitted to the atmosphere as it burns (Benscoter et al., 2011). Peatland's ecosystem is an amazing process that prevents disastrous wildfires due to its fire-resistant nature. Therefore, peatlands play an essential role in helping preserve the health of the planet.

The impacts of climate change on peatlands

As the Earth warms, the effects of climate change are apparent on peatlands. Climate change will alter the basic characteristics of peatlands including their wetness, nutrient shortages, and relations to the cold environment. Warm temperatures induce the growth of vascular plants due to increased mineralization, nitrogen, and phosphorus availability. These vascular plants such as dwarf shrubs, ferns, conifers, and flowering plants. While people may think the growth of more shrubs and various plants is great for the environment due to more photosynthesis reactions, it is extremely harmful to the peatland ecosystem. These vascular plants suppress the growth of endangered plant species, such as moss and lichens, which thrive in phosphorus-limited environments. Decreasing the number of these endangered plant species, will ultimately lead to a change in vegetation composition and decrease the peatland biodiversity (Bu et al., 2011). The response of peat decay to global warming shows that there are higher peat decomposition rates as the mean annual temperature increases (Clymo et al., 1998). 90% of peat organic carbon in the deep layer peatlands and 40% in the shallow layer peatlands would no longer exist if the Earth's temperature increased by 4°C during dry periods (Ise et al., 2008; Bu et al., 2011). These decomposition rates, however, vary from different peat-related species. For example, in warmer periods, Sphagnum peat decay rates remain low because of their low nitrogen content and cellular composition. Similarly, other major peat-forming species, S.fuscum and S.magellanicum, decompose very slowly because they distribute more carbon in structural carbohydrates, thus, not reacting to the global warming effects (Turetsky, et al., 2008).

A study displayed that under winter conditions, carbon dioxide emissions under deep snow treatments were twice as large as under regular ambient temperatures (Jones et al., 1998). In regions with permafrost and seasonal frost, climate changes' increasing temperatures could result in the oxidation and decomposition of formerly frozen peat. Peatlands responding to global warming began increasing the coverage of Sphagnum moss, which increased peat accumulation (Bu et al., 2011; Turetsky et al., 2007). The positive outcome of increased peat formation is only temporary because eventually, the peatland will lose its original environmental characteristics to slowly accumulate peat. Thereby, displaying a negative response to climate change (Dise, 2009; Bu et al., 2011).

The change in environmental composition will also increase the flux of methane and even carbon dioxide. As mentioned earlier, peatlands are the Earth's natural carbon stocks and carbon sinks that help reduce carbon emissions from the atmosphere. While peatlands serve this vital purpose in the Earth's ecosystem, these wetlands may be aggravating global warming by contributing to the emission of greenhouse gases like carbon dioxide, methane, and nitrous oxide. Peatlands become a carbon source instead of a carbon sink. They have the potential to increase air temperature through greenhouse gas emissions but can also decrease air temperature by consuming carbon dioxide and creating more peat. Studies found that peatlands' net primary productivity and peat accumulation increase with global warming in permafrost peatlands (Camill et al., 2001). Other studies found that in the boreal zone, peatlands' carbon sink function is maintained with the help of climate warming (Vitt et al., 2000; Flanagan & Syed, 2011). But these positive reactions to climate change are not long-lasting as many of the peatlands' original environmental characteristics are lost due to climate adaptation. Instead, peat decay rates would significantly increase and these peatlands would no longer serve their original purpose as carbon sinks, but rather, as carbon sources (Malmer et al., 2005). Therefore, generating positive feedback to further aggravate the climate crisis.

While it is evident that peatlands help break out-of-control fires, the opposite is true for dried peatlands. More than 90% of peatlands are found in high-latitude regions, making them more susceptible to wildfires. Degraded peatlands are shown to intensify and prolong uncontrollable fires due to the carbon-rich nature of this unique ecosystem (Turestky et al., 2011). These immense wildfires also place an economic toll on countries. For instance, in 2010, Russia experienced a large peatland fire which resulted in $15 billion US in damage and reduced industrial output (Goldhammer, 2010; Kim & Levitov, 2010). Since peatlands store lots of carbon, the degradation and overexploitation of peatlands release immense quantities of greenhouse gasses. According to the International Union for Conservation of Nature, there is an estimated 1.9 gigatonnes of carbon dioxide emissions released from drained peatlands annually. This amount is equivalent to 5% of global anthropogenic greenhouse gas emissions. Forest fires in Indonesian peat swamps emitted almost 16 million tonnes of carbon dioxide daily back in 2015 (ICUN, 2022). The number of peatland fires will only begin to increase due to the drastic effects of climate change including an increase in temperatures, extreme changes in precipitation levels, an increase in frequencies of droughts, and increases in the length of fire seasons. The average daily summer temperatures are projected to increase by 1.5-2.5°C in peatland-fertile areas like Canada's boreal region. While precipitation is expected to increase by 20% in eastern Canada, western regions where most peatlands are situated are not going to endure precipitation (Turestky et al., 2011). These conditions cultivate a recipe for intense peatland fires.

It is determined that the continual growth of spruce trees in drained peatlands further harms the peatland's ability to stay resistant to fire. When left unchecked, these trees continue to grow tall and wide, which shields Sphagnum, a special fire-resistant moss, from growing. Not only do these enormous trees prevent Sphagnum growth, but they also absorb immense quantities of water due to the size of these trees. Instead of helping absorb carbon dioxide in the atmosphere, these giant spruce trees serve as a giant straw that sucks up all the water from the peat. Thereby, creating a forest filled with large trees and years of stored carbon in dry peat ready to burn (Waddington & Wilkinson, 2022).

Consequences of peatland degradation

In general, degraded ecosystems can deteriorate to meet a critical threshold wherein small alterations in that environment eventually leads to large changes in the condition, function, and state of the ecosystem. Degradation includes draining an ecosystem, like peatlands, for human usage. Draining peatlands leads to peat oxidation, amplified carbon dioxide emissions, and changes in plant communities that will fully change the carbon and water equilibrium in this ecosystem. Peatland degradation due to change in land usage and drainage for agricultural purposes is responsible for 5 to 10% of global anthropogenic carbon dioxide emissions every year. The consequences of peatland degradation are evident in the following outcomes: (1) alteration in peat structure, (2) decrease in plant diversity, and (3) human health consequences.

Alteration in peat structure

The formation of peat is a slow and long process that consists of accumulating organic-rich and partly decomposed plant material. This results in the development of a unique soil composition that decelerates the movement of water across different peatland basins. Due to the loose and less decomposed nature of the upper layers of the soil matrix, this portion can retain excess water– which is useful during dry periods as the upper layers release the stored water to the deeper peats. Similarly, in an event of excess water from rain or snow/ice melts, the water surplus can be released to nearby streams. This helps maintain a sufficient water table in case of drought or extremely dry weather (Losiel & Gallego-Sala, 2022).

However, when a peatland is drained or altered, decomposition rates rise. This results in denser solids and decreased soil porosity—porosity is essential in allowing for the movement of water and nutrients to the soil (Indoria et al., 2020). Continuous draining of peat over decades may result in desiccation (the removal of moisture), soil instability, more fluctuations in the water table, and erosion. These outcomes will lead to an increase in rapid runoff during and after precipitation, which results in water pollution and possibly urban flooding (depending on the neighbouring area). Moreover, peatland drainage uses intense and prolonged drying which leads to cracks in peat, increasing the subsurface flow. The exposure to oxygen promotes soil decomposition, which leads to net carbon, water, and biodiversity loss due to hydrological instability. Therefore, degradation will lead to irreversible changes in peat structure, thus, destabilizing the ecosystem (Losiel & Gallego-Sala, 2022).

Decrease in plant diversity

Studies have shown that the more biologically diverse and ecosystem is, the more resilient it is (Ives & Carpenter, 2007). The environmental characteristics of peatlands have created great biodiversity among plants and microorganisms. Many of these species have adapted physiologically and metabolically to their low oxygen environment, cold temperature, acidity, and low nutrient availability (oligotrophy). As mentioned in the previous subchapters, plants like Sphagnum can hold up to 20 times their dry weight in water to survive during dry periods. This moss is also great at colonizing or recovering areas due to its spores that can spread over long distances and how it acidifies its environment to prevent other plants from colonizing the area. Unfortunately, with peat drainage, plant diversity decreases. Due to the hydrological changes and loss of original soil characteristics, it is difficult for Sphagnum and other peatland mosses to recolonize. This decrease in plant biodiversity affects the way the peatland copes with climate change (Losiel & Gallego-Sala, 2022).

Human health consequences

The air pollution emitted from the peatland fires not only worsened the climate crisis for years but also greatly impacted the health of people living near these fires. Indonesian peatlands have been drained for the sake of agricultural development for several decades which has significantly helped the development of their economy. However, the draining of peatlands has made these lands more susceptible to intense peatland fires, which resulted in the emission of toxic air pollution. Researchers found that in Indonesia, 33 100 adults and 2 900 infants die prematurely annually from air pollution in general. Moreover, peatland fires cause 4 400 additional hospitalizations related to respiratory diseases, 635 000 severe cases of asthma in children, and 8.9 million lost workdays (Hein et al., 2022). These numbers will only increase as the temperature warms and the duration and prominence of wildfires continue to expand. Despite the Indonesian economy improving through the decades due to agricultural developments, the drainage of peatlands is not worth it if thousands of people are dying due to air pollution and the health of hundreds upon thousands of individuals are severely impacted due to emergencies of peatland fires.

Canadian Peatland Restoration

Twenty years of peatland restoration experiments and monitoring Canadian peatlands have provided scientists with an adequate and efficient technique to restore drained and degraded peatlands. Scientists have demonstrated, using the Moss Layer Transfer Technique, that Sphagnum cover can be reestablished very quickly– within four growing seasons. Scientists reintroduce Sphagnum mosses, specifically Sphagnum Acutifolia, back into the degraded peatlands due to its high moisture retention capacity and rapidly restore the carbon accumulation function of restored peatlands. Other studies have shown the benefits of restoration, many of which include the increasing return of moss coverage, stable and high-water table conditions, net carbon sequestration (a practice involving the removal of carbon from the atmosphere and storing it), and resistance to wildfire (Losiel & Gallego-Sala, 2022).

Projected Peatland Models for Long-Term Assessment

As climate change continues to dry out the boreal region, the threat of peatland fires and carbon loss continues to grow. Several studies investigated peatland protection and restoration for climate change mitigation using projected models (Bridgham et al., 2008; Humpenöder et al., 2020). One study assessed the consequences of peatland degradation along with the increasing global demand for food and a growing population. This study also explored the effects on food security when implementing peatland protection and restoration policies for lowering greenhouse gas emissions from degraded peatlands. The researchers created three different scenarios: (1) no peatland policy, (2) peatland protection policy), and (3) peatland protection and restoration policy.

The results from the three scenarios showed that the scenario without peatland policies displayed a 22% increase in the global degraded peatland area within the next century. With the tropical peatlands being the most impacted. As a result of the degraded peatlands, the annual global carbon dioxide emissions increased by 25% by the year 2100. In the second scenario with the peatland protection policy, the number of degraded peatlands will increase only slightly within the next century. The increase in peatland emissions in this scenario is mainly due to the legacy of historic and preexisting peatland degradation. The third scenario depicting the peatland protection and restoration policy displays a substantial decrease in degraded peatland areas due to rewetting land by the year 2100. This corresponds to a 60% decrease in degraded peatlands. Restoring 50% of the degraded peatlands through the rewetting system, required only a decade of operation, meaning that it is a cost-efficient form of climate mitigation measure using low carbon dioxide prices. However, due to the restoration system of peatlands, methane emissions more than doubled within the century. But despite the doubling of methane emissions, because of the extremely low carbon dioxide emissions from restored peatlands and higher carbon sink via vegetation regrowth, the Earth turns into a global net carbon sink by 2075. Thereby, returning to its healthy natural environmental state by the end of the 21st century (Humpenöder et al., 2020).

Implications of future peatland protection and restoration

Based on Humpenöder and the company's models, creating peatland protection and restoration policies is crucial for the health of the planet. As a result, this future process will affect other aspects involving socioeconomics and plant trade-offs.

Socioeconomic impacts

While it is cost-efficient to restore degraded peatlands as they impact only a small area of land, these measures may have economic impacts. Simply because this implies the expansion of managed land, which may increase the overall cost of agricultural production. Based on empirical evidence, the protection and restoration of peatlands affect lowering greenhouse gas emissions but have little to no effect on agricultural production costs and food prices (Humpenöder et al., 2020).

Plant trade-offs

A recent study showed that wetland degradation results in plant dwarfism and can even hinder the life history of plants; all of which are closely associated with eco-physiological processes and nutritional requirements of plants (Zhang et al., 2022). The restoration of wetlands can change degraded habitats by promoting plant growth and improving the community biomass. Peatland restoration can alleviate the soil environment and improve nutrient degradation (Wang et al., 2020).

However, a study found that rewetting drained peatlands induce the growth of tall grass-like (graminoids) wetland plants, and the biodiverse ecosystem species that once inhabited the lands originally ceased to exist for at least several decades. These have implications beyond simply biodiversity. The composition of plant species affects the Earth's carbon cycle through litter quality, production, and consumption of carbon in the atmosphere, all of which impact gas emissions. Brown mosses, vital plants in the peatland ecosystem, are greatly absent in rewetted peatlands due to the domination of graminoids (Losiel & Gallego-Sala, 2022).

Conclusion

According to the Paris Agreement, the treaty aims for carbon neutrality by 2050 to 2070, within the next thirty to fifty years (IPCC, 2022). This means that it is crucial that as scientists, policy-makers, workers, and global citizens the international objective is to reach this goal of carbon neutrality for the sake of generations to come. This means cutting greenhouse gas emissions using Earth's largest natural carbon storage facility, peatlands. Peatlands are a sacred and vital ecosystem that exists naturally only on this planet. Despite being limited in size when compared to the Earth's land surface area, the purpose of peatlands is of great essence. The consequences of degrading this vital carbon storage unit are detrimental to its environmental peat structure, plant biodiversity, and most importantly, human health. Without this ecosystem, humans have lost a vital natural resource to help mitigate the current climate crisis. Scientists have spent over twenty years analyzing and creating projected models for peatlands. As a result of their analysis and calculations, they have concluded that by restoring and protecting peatlands through Moss Layer Transfer Techniques and implementation of protection policies, Earth will have restored its natural atmospheric state by the end of the century. Therefore, after assessing the benefits and drawbacks of peatland restoration and degradation, it is notably evident that the pros outweigh the cons. What cannot be replaced is the natural health and state of the only habitable planet known to humankind– thus far.

References

Benscoter, B. W., Thompson, D. K., Waddington, J. M., Flannigan, M. D., Wotton, B. M., De Groot, W. J., & Turetsky, M. R. (2011).

Interactive effects of vegetation, soil moisture, and bulk density on the depth of burning of thick organic soils. International Journal of Wildland Fire, 20(3), 418. doi: 10.1071/wf08183

Bu, Z., Hans, J., Li, H., Zhao, G., Zheng, X., Ma, J., & Zeng, J. (2011). The response of peatlands to climate warming: A Review. Acta Ecologica Sinica, 31(3), 157-162. doi: 10.1016/j. chnaes.2011.03.006

Camill, P., Lynch, J. A., Clark, J. S., Adams, J. B., & Jordan, B. (2001). Changes in biomass, aboveground net primary production, and peat accumulation following permafrost thaw in the boreal peatlands of Manitoba, Canada. Ecosystems, 4(5), 461-478. doi: 10.1007/s10021-001-0022-3

Clymo, R. S., Turunen, J., & Tolonen, K. (1998). Carbon accumulation in Peatland. Oikos, 81(2), 368. doi: 10.2307/3547057

Dise, N. B. (2009). Peatland Response to Global Change. Science, 326(5954), 810-811. doi: 10.1126/science.1174268

Flanagan, L. B., & Syed, K. H. (2011). Stimulation of both photosynthesis and respiration in response to warmer and drier conditions in a boreal peatland ecosystem. Global Change Biology, 17(7), 2271-2287. doi: 10.1111/j.1365-2486.2010.02378.x

Goldhammer, J. G. (2010, August 15). Preliminary assessment of the fire situation in Western Russia 2010. Retrieved from https:// gfmc.online/wp-content/uploads/Russia-1-1.pdf

Hein, L., Spadaro, J. V., Ostro, B., Hammer, M., Sumarga, E., Salmayenti, R., & Castañeda, J. (2022). The health impacts of Indonesian peatland fires. Environmental Health, 21(1). doi: 10.1186/s12940-022-00872-w

Humpenöder, F., Karstens, K., Lotze-Campen, H., Leifeld, J., Menichetti, L., Barthelmes, A., & Popp, A. (2020). Peatland

Protection and Restoration Are Key for climate change mitigation. Environmental Research Letters, 15(10), 104093. doi: 10.1088/1748-9326/abae2a

ICUN. (2022, November 02). Peatlands and climate change. Retrieved from https://www.iucn.org/resources/issues-brief/peatlands-and-climate-change

Indoria, A. K., Sharma, K. L., & Reddy, K. S. (2020). Hydraulic properties of soil under Warming Climate. Climate Change and Soil Interactions, 473-508. doi: 10.1016/b978-0-12-818032-7.00018-7

IPCC. (2022). Global Warming of 1.5°C. Retrieved from https://www.ipcc.ch/sr15/download/#full

IPS. (2020, September 22). Where can peatlands be found? Retrieved from https://peatlands.org/peatlands/where-can-peatlands-be-found/

Ise, T., Dunn, A. L., Wofsy, S. C., & Moorcroft, P. R. (2008). High sensitivity of peat decomposition to climate change through water-table feedback. Nature Geoscience, 1(11), 763-766. doi: 10.1038/ngeo331

Ives, A. R., & Carpenter, S. R. (2007). Stability and diversity of ecosystems. Science, 317(5834), 58-62. doi: 10.1126/science.1133258

Jones, M. H., Fahnestock, J. T., Walker, D. A., Walker, M. D., & Welker, J. M. (1998). Carbon dioxide fluxes in moist and dry arctic tundra during the snow-free season: Responses to increases in summer temperature and winter snow accumulation. Arctic and Alpine Research, 30(4), 373-380. doi: 10.1080/00040851.1998.12002912

Joosten, H. (2015). Peatlands, climate change mitigation, and biodiversity conservation: An issue brief on the importance of peatlands for carbon and biodiversity conservation and the role of drained peatlands as greenhouse gas emission hotspots: Policy brief (pp. 4-6). Copenhagen: Nordic Council of Ministers. doi: 10.6027/ANP2015-727

Joosten, H., & Clarke, D. (2002). Wise use of Mires and peatlands: Background and principles including a framework for decision-making. Totnes: International Mire Conservation Group.

Kim, L., & Levitov, M. (2010, August 10). Russia's heat may cost 15,000 lives, and $15 billion of GDP. Retrieved from https://www.bloomberg.com/news/articles/2010-08-10/russia-may-lose-15-000-lives-15-billion-of-economic-output-in-heat-wave

Loisel, J., & Gallego-Sala, A. (2022). Ecological resilience of restored peatlands to climate change. Communications, Earth & Environment, 3(1). doi: 10.1038/s43247-022-00547-x

Malmer, N., Johansson, T., Olsrud, M., & Christensen, T. R. (2005). Vegetation, climatic changes and net carbon sequestration in a north-Scandinavian subarctic mire over 30 years. Global Change Biology, 0(0). doi: 10.1111/j.1365-2486.2005.01042.x

Turetsky, M. R., Crow, S. E., Evans, R. J., Vitt, D. H., & Wieder, R. K. (2008). Trade-offs in resource allocation among moss species control decomposition in boreal peatlands. Journal of Ecology, 96(6), 1297-1305. doi: 10.1111/j.1365-2745.2008.01438.x

Turetsky, M. R., Wieder, R. K., Vitt, D. H., Evans, R. J., & Scott, K. D. (2007). The disappearance of relict permafrost in Boreal North America: Effects on Peatland Carbon Storage and fluxes. Global Change Biology, 13(9), 1922-1934. doi: 10.1111/j.1365-2486.2007.01381.x

Turetsky, M., Donahue, W., & Benscoter, B. (2011). Experimental drying intensifies burning and carbon losses in a northern peatland. Nature Communications, 2(1). doi:10.1038/ncomms1523

UK Centre for Ecology & Hydrology. (n.d.). Peatlands factsheet - UK centre for ecology & hydrology. Retrieved from https://www. ceh.ac.uk/sites/default/files/Peatland%20factsheet.pdf

Vitt, D. H., Halsey, L. A., Bauer, I. E., & Campbell, C. (2000). Spatial and temporal trends in carbon storage of peatlands of continental western Canada through the Holocene. Canadian Journal of Earth Sciences, 37(5), 683-693. doi: 10.1139/e99-097

Waddington, M., & Wilkinson, S. (2022, November 03). How to fight wildfires and climate change with wetlands. Retrieved from https://theconversation.com/how-to-fight-wildfires-and-climate-change-with-wetlands-117356

Wang, G., Jiang, M., Wang, M., & Xue, Z. (2020). Element composition of soils to assess the success of Wetland Restoration. Land Degradation & Development, 31(13), 1641-1649. doi:10.1002/ldr.3561

Xu, J., Morris, P. J., Liu, J., & Holden, J. (2018). PEATMAP: Refining estimates of global peatland distribution based on a meta-analysis. CATENA, 160(1), 134-140. doi: 10.1016/j.catena.2017.09.010

Zhang, D., Xia, J., Sun, J., Dong, K., Shao, P., Wang, X., & Tong, S. (2022). Effect of wetland restoration and degradation on nutrient trade-off of Carex Schmidtii. Frontiers in Ecology and Evolution, 9. doi: 10.3389/fevo.2021.801608

Chapter 3
Adaptation to Crops

Hafsa Binte Younus

Introduction

Agriculture is the art and science of cultivating crops and livestock (The art and science of agriculture, n.d.). It provides most of the world's food and fabric. Agricultural production, especially the production of crops, is highly dependent on weather and climate as these factors have a huge impact on other factors such as soil content and quality, temperature, and water availability. Without appropriate rainfall, temperatures, and other factors, crops fail (The art and science of agriculture, n.d.).

The effects of climate change have been accelerating significantly over the last century. An increase in extreme weather events and changes and weather conditions have been observed as the Earth's climate continues to move toward the warmer side (Calleja-Cabrera et al., 2020). It is predicted that by 2050 there will be an increase in the global mean temperature by around 1.5 to 2° C (Calleja-Cabrera et al., 2020). Moreover, alterations to climate such as the increased frequency of heat waves, fewer days of freezing temperatures, and an overall lower quantity but more intense precipitation have been predicted (Calleja-Cabrera et al., 2020). Such extreme temperature and weather changes will negatively impact agricultural production (Calleja-Cabrera et al., 2020).

In the coming years, more food will be needed to feed the population as it is expected that by 2050 there will be an increase in population by around 2 billion people (Calleja-Cabrera et al., 2020). However, the negative impact of climate change on crop production where the loss of crop yield is predicted has been a concern for food security (Calleja-Cabrera et al., 2020). It is expected that by 2050 without effective adaptive measures in place, there will be a decrease in the yield of crops by 30% (Hobert & Negra, 2020). This is why, even though different geographical locations will be impacted differently to various degrees, it is extremely important to maintain and improve the productivity of crops under climate constraints (Calleja-Cabrera et al., 2020).

This chapter will explore the impact of climate change on crops along with some adaptation techniques which include adaptation through developing appropriate root traits, adaptation through crop migration, and adaptation through biodiversity.

Impact of Climate Change on Crops

Factors such as changes in temperature, atmospheric carbon dioxide (CO_2) levels, as well as the frequency and intensity of extreme weather have a significant impact on the yield of crops (Climate Impacts on Agriculture and Food Supply, n.d.). However, the degree of impact of these factors depends on the crop's optimal temperature for growth and reduction (Climate Impacts on Agriculture and Food Supply, n.d.). For example, warming may benefit crops that are typically grown in warmer areas, however, that same higher temperature that exceeds a crop's optimum temperature results in a decline in the yield of the crop (Climate Impacts on Agriculture and Food Supply, n.d.).

The increase in temperature is one of the aspects of climate change that the world is currently dealing with (Gornall et al., 2010). This increase in temperature can significantly impact agricultural productivity, farm income, and food security (Gornall et al., 2010). Although an increase in temperature is associated with an increase in the productivity of crops at mid and high altitudes such as cereals and cool-season seed crops (Gornall et al., 2010). Crops such as a maze, sunflower, and soybean which are prevalent in southern Europe could also be liable further in the North and higher altitudes as a result of high temperature. The yield of these crops could increase to as much as 30% by 2050 (Gornall et al., 2010). On the other hand, in geographical locations where the temperatures are already close to the physiological maxima of the crop, such an increase in temperature could be detrimental as it may increase the heat stress on the crops and also result in a higher water loss by evaporation (Gornall et al., 2010). For example, a 2° increase in temperature could result in an increase in reproduction by 10% at high latitudes however at low latitudes that same increase would result in a decrease in the yield of wheat by nearly the same amount (Gornall et al., 2010). Therefore, if correct adaptations are not put in place, even moderate levels of climate change may not necessarily confer benefits and may overall reduce the final lead of the crops (Gornall et al., 2010). Increasing temperatures also pose a huge risk to the yield of crops because many weeds, pests, and fungi thrive under warmer temperatures along with an increased CO2 level (Climate Impacts on Agriculture and Food Supply, n.d.). Climate change is also associated with a likely increase in weeds and pests. The increase in weeds and pests has also been reported to be related to the decline in crop yield (Climate Impacts on Agriculture and Food Supply, n.d.). This is because weed competes with crops for light, water, and nutrients. Currently, US farmers spend more than 11 billion dollars per year to fight weeds. However, the increase in the use of pesticides is a threat to human health (Climate Impacts on Agriculture and Food Supply, n.d.).

The uncertainty around water available for crops is another factor that comes with climate change. Over 80% of the total agriculture is rainfed (Gornall et al., 2010). The impact of global warming on precipitation is difficult to predict (Gornall et al., 2010). This is because there are a few key factors that affect the level of precipitation which include atmospheric water content and dynamic monsoon circulation (Gornall et al., 2010). However, water availability is not just influenced by precipitation but is also heavily dependent on the increase in evaporative demand for water due to rising temperatures (Gornall et al., 2010). It is estimated that there would be an increase in the crop irrigation requirement globally by around 5 to 20% due to increasing evaporative demand for water and longer growing seasons. It is estimated that the irrigation requirements could increase by 15% in the Southeast Asian region as well as North African and Middle Eastern regions (Gornall et al., 2010). However, there would be a decrease in demand in China (Gornall et al., 2010).

The level of carbon dioxide also affects crop yields (Climate Impacts on Agriculture and Food Supply, n.d.). In today's world, the rise in CO_2 levels has been observed due to the increase in the cutting of trees and forests because of industrialization and urbanization. Studies have shown that an elevated level of CO_2 results in an increase in plant growth (Climate Impacts on Agriculture and Food Supply, n.d.). However, the side effects of increased CO_2 such as changes in temperature, ozone, water, and nutrient constraints may counteract the potential increase in yield (Climate Impacts on Agriculture and Food Supply, n.d.). For example, elevated CO_2 levels have been associated with reduced protein and nitrogen content in alfalfa and soybean plants resulting in a decrease in their quality (Climate Impacts on Agriculture and Food Supply, n.d.). Elevated CO_2 levels are also associated with a reduction in the nutritional value of most food crops (Climate Impacts on Agriculture and Food Supply, n.d.). This is because increased atmospheric carbon dioxide levels result in a reduction in the concentration of protein and essential minerals in most plant species including rice, soybean, and wheat (Climate Impacts on Agriculture and Food Supply, n.d.). This decrease in the nutritional value of crops is then associated with a potential threat to human health (Climate Impacts on Agriculture and Food Supply, n.d.).

Adaptation by Roots

Adaptation refers to the action taken to reduce the impact of damages and to make full use of beneficial opportunities (Sloat et al., 2020). As discussed, climate change is a threat to productivity around the world and new solutions are needed to adapt crops to these environmental changes. Elevated temperature affects developmental and physiological plant processes which then eventually impact the crop yield and quality (Calleja-Cabrera, Boter, Oñate-Sánchez, & Pernas, 2020). One of the most important factors involved in the survival and quality of crops is the crop's water and nutrient uptake (Calleja-Cabrera, Boter, Oñate-Sánchez, & Pernas, 2020). These processes are performed by the roots of the plant (Calleja-Cabrera, Boter, Oñate-Sánchez, & Pernas, 2020). However, changes in the soil temperature, as well as the soil content due to climate change, limit the growth of the crops (Calleja-Cabrera, Boter, Oñate-Sánchez, & Pernas, 2020). This is because at higher temperatures plants have a higher water demand due to the increased loss of water by evaporation and a decrease in water uptake by the roots (Calleja-Cabrera, Boter, Oñate-Sánchez, & Pernas, 2020). Water uptake in the roots takes place either through aquaporins which are membrane channels that facilitate water transport or by diffusion through the plasmatic membrane (Calleja-Cabrera, Boter, Oñate-Sánchez, & Pernas, 2020). At high temperatures, crops have different responses of aquaporin and plasma membrane fluidity in roots (Calleja-Cabrera, Boter, Oñate-Sánchez, & Pernas, 2020). For example, in pepper and wheat plants aquaporin activity is positively associated with water uptake and warmer soils.

However, in broccoli aquaporin activity is negatively impacted by warmer temperatures as the quantity and activity of aquaporin decreases in the roots of that plant (Calleja-Cabrera, Boter, Oñate-Sánchez, & Pernas, 2020). Nutrient balance is also impacted by changes in temperature. Similar to the crop aquaporin activity, nutrient uptake also varies from crop to crop (Calleja-Cabrera, Boter, Oñate-Sánchez, & Pernas, 2020). For example, in tomato crops, warmer soil limits root growth which then results in a decrease in nutrient uptake causing a decrease in macro and micronutrient levels in the crop (Calleja-Cabrera, Boter, Oñate-Sánchez, & Pernas, 2020). On the contrary, in agrostis stolonifera which is a grass species used to feed livestock, high-temperature results in a lower number of roots and increased uptake and partitioning of nitrogen, phosphorus, and potassium (Calleja-Cabrera, Boter, Oñate-Sánchez, & Pernas, 2020). From these examples, it can be seen that roots respond differently to increases in temperature in different crops (Calleja-Cabrera, Boter, Oñate-Sánchez, & Pernas, 2020). Therefore, one solution to limit this negative impact of climate change could be to develop efficient root systems (by breeding) which would then allow the crop to better adapt to the changing soil and environmental conditions (Calleja-Cabrera, Boter, Oñate-Sánchez, & Pernas, 2020). Developing appropriate root traits associated with improved adaptation to rising temperatures could help improve crop yield and quality.

Adaptation by Crop Migration

Another way of crop adaptation to climate change is crop migration. Data from 1973 to 2012 has shown that rainfed crop yields (maize, rice, wheat, and soybean) have been negatively affected by rising temperatures due to climate change (Sloat et al., 2020). Crop migration has mediated crop growing season temperatures (Sloat et al., 2020). Studies have shown that compared to the 1970s, today rainfed crops are experiencing temperatures that are much hotter than before (Sloat et al., 2020). However today the degree of extreme temperature exposure to crops has been modified by changing harvested areas through crop migration (Sloat et al., 2020). This has allowed for the 95th percentile of the temperature of rain-fed crop environments to now actually be cooler than in 1975 (Sloat et al., 2020). This would not have been the case without adaptation through crop migration as wheat would have experienced a larger upper boundary temperature increase instead of the largest decrease that it is experiencing today due to the movement of harvested areas and expansion of irrigation (Sloat et al., 2020). In terms of wheat adaptation through migration, the wheat crop has been shifted out to some of the coldest areas of Canada and Russia (Sloat et al., 2020). This resulted in rainfed wheat being able to grow in an overall more favorable temperature which would not have been the case without changes to distribution and irrigation (Sloat et al., 2020).

In warmer regions like South Asia, irrigation expansion has resulted in aiding wheat farming (Sloat et al., 2020). Another example of crops that benefited through crop migration includes maze crops (Sloat et al., 2020). In North America, Maze crops have been shifted away from the American Southeast towards the upper Midwest (Sloat et al., 2020). There, farmers planted a variety of crops to benefit from the longer growing seasons and less frequent extreme heat. Rainfed rice crops have also been moved to slightly cooler environments to avoid high-temperature exposures as well as increase rice irrigation in the warmest part of its range including Brazil, Spain, India as well as China (Sloat et al., 2020). Studies done by Wang and Hijmans reported that in China an overall benefit to nationwide yields of rice was reported as a result of the northward geographic expansion of rice crops to adapt to climate changes (Sloat et al., 2020).

Crops are not just migrated from hotter climates to cooler climates. Adaptation to climate change by migrating crops from cooler climates to warmer climates has also increased crop production (Sloat et al., 2020). For example, rainfed soybean crops have benefited from the higher temperatures in locations such as India and Brazil and there is an overall increase in yield by 158% (Sloat et al., 2020). The development of new soybean varieties has also allowed for this increase in yields. The increase in this crop was way more compared to the other three crops discussed above (Sloat et al., 2020).

On the contrary, crop migrations also have limitations and side effects. For example, continuous crop migration can impact biodiversity, use of land, socioeconomic situations, as well as agricultural activity (Sloat et al., 2020). Moreover, all crop migration is also dependent on the expansion of irrigation. Crop migration also has environmental impacts such as a reduction in carbon storage, depletion of the color of water, reduction of wildlife habitat, as well as a decrease in biodiversity (Sloat et al., 2020). This is why a continued shift in crop production may not always be the most suitable climate adaptation for developing countries (Sloat et al., 2020). For example, in South America, an increase in soybean production has resulted in a damaging impact on its Cerrado biome, which is home to a variety of ecosystems (Sloat et al., 2020). Moreover, an increase in irrigation can also be a problematic strategy used for adaptation to climate (Sloat et al., 2020). This is because an increase in irrigation can negatively impact water resources as it can post stress on water supplies and overall result in a decrease in water quality (Sloat et al., 2020).

Regardless of its limitations, crop migration is an effective adaptation strategy as it has aided in elevating the effect of high temperatures on the world's staple crops such as wheat, rice, and maze (Sloat et al., 2020).

Adaptation by Biodiversity

One of the longer-term adaptations of agricultural ecosystems includes the biodiversity of cultivated species (Anne-Céline & Yves, 2021). This is a combination of several species in a crop. From an agricultural point of view, there is only a small portion of species of plants that contribute to the world's planned production. Out of 391,000 known vascularized plant species only around 31,000 are used by humans and only around 5,000 are consumed through diets (Anne-Céline & Yves, 2021). However, when comparing the countries of the South, it is revealed that the 50 countries that are least developed contained four times more agricultural biodiversity as compared to all the other countries present on the planet (Anne-Céline & Yves, 2021). Centers of domestication which give rise to today's cultivated plants live within these well-diversified areas (Anne-Céline & Yves, 2021). These cultivated plants grow close to their wild ancestors allowing for gene flow to be possible and therefore allowing for local maintenance of a continuous supply of diversity within the cultivated compartment. The reason biodiversity is important is that it allows for an insurance effect to exist (Anne-Céline & Yves, 2021). This is because it allows for the cultivation of a large number of different species which are not equally sensitive to environmental variations (Anne-Céline & Yves, 2021). This way more diversified cultivation of species can guarantee that the overall level of production would be less affected by climate changes and hazards as compared to when only one species is cultivated (Anne-Céline & Yves, 2021). Moreover, biodiversity also allows for complementary logical niches which means that the species together optimized the use of resources which eventually leads to better use of resources and an overall higher overall production and yield (Anne-Céline & Yves, 2021).

Another benefit of biodiversity is that it allows for beneficial nutrient input into the crop (Anne-Céline & Yves, 2021). This way the nutrient supply which is needed or beneficial for the cultivation of one plant can be generated by another plant and this phenomenon is called facilitation (Anne-Céline & Yves, 2021). For example, by planting leguminous plants and cereals together, fewer fertilizers are needed to be used by the farmers as the nitrogen fixed in the air and added to the soil by the leguminous plants is used by cereal plant crops (Anne-Céline & Yves, 2021). Moreover, a 10-year field study in Malawi showed that the combination of peanut or soybean plants with maize improved yield (Anne-Céline & Yves, 2021).

High genetic diversity also allows for local adaptation. In extreme conditions or when responding to environmental pressures or other selection pressures, having high genetic diversities allows farmers to select varieties that are better adapted to those conditions (Anne-Céline & Yves, 2021). It allows the farmers to overlay natural selection with decisive androgenic factors to maintain the dynamic of their crop diversity based on the response of the crop to the environment (Anne-Céline & Yves, 2021). This process of human selection and natural environmental selection allows for the continuous evolution of varieties which then leads to the adaptation of different species to different climates (Anne-Céline & Yves, 2021). An example of this includes the maze crop which is a naturally tropical plant that grows at low altitudes. However, through recent local adaptations, millet crops have been seen in Niger which have earlier flowering as a response to more drought over the period (Anne-Céline & Yves, 2021).

Conclusion

Overall, it has been noted that climate change has negatively impacted agricultural production. This is why crop adaptation to climate change is extremely important, especially the production of crops, to ensure food security for the growing population. Although some methods such as adaptation through developing appropriate root traits, crop migration, and through biodiversity are being implemented, more research is needed to develop effective measures and practices to adapt crops to the changing climates and ensure food security in the future.

References

Anne-Céline, T., & Yves, V. (2021, November 24). Biodiversity and crop adaptation to climate change in developing countries. Retrieved from https://www.encyclopedie-environnement.org/en/life/biodiversity-crop-adaptation-to-climate-change-in-developing-countries/

Calleja-Cabrera, J., Boter, M., Oñate-Sánchez, L., & Pernas, M. (2020). Root growth adaptation to climate change in crops. Frontiers in Plant Science, 11. doi:10.3389/fpls.2020.00544

Climate Impacts on Agriculture and Food Supply. (n.d.). Retrieved from https://climatechange.chicago.gov/climate-impacts/climate-impacts-agriculture-and-food-supply

Gornall, J., Betts, R., Burke, E., Clark, R., Camp, J., Willett, K., & Wiltshire, A. (2010).

Implications of climate change for agricultural productivity in the early twenty-first century. Philosophical Transactions of the Royal Society B: Biological Sciences, 365(1554), 2973-2989. doi:10.1098/rstb.2010.0158

Hobert, R., & Negra, C. (2020, September 1). Climate change and the future of food | unfoundation.org. Retrieved from https://unfoundation.org/blog/post/climate-change-and-the-future-of-food/

Sloat, L. L., Davis, S. J., Gerber, J. S., Moore, F. C., Ray, D. K., West, P. C., & Mueller, N. D. (2020). Climate adaptation by Crop Migration. Nature Communications, 11(1). doi:10.1038/s41467-020-15076-4

The art and science of agriculture. (n.d.). Retrieved from https://education.nationalgeographic.org/resource/agriculture

Chapter 4
Infrastructure
Mahnoor Irfan

Introduction

Climate change is having an impact on the ecosystem all around the world, from fires in the Amazon and Australia to flash flooding in Europe. But how does climate change affect critical infrastructure, and how does infrastructure affect our climate?

Infrastructure is responsible for 79 percent of all greenhouse gas emissions and 88 percent of all adaptation costs, it is critical to meeting the Paris Agreement and the Sustainable Development Goals (UNEP, 2021). Extreme heat can cause road buckling, while freeze-thaw cycles can cause pavement cracking and potholes. Extreme weather increases weather unpredictability, and roads designed for a specific temperature range may fail more quickly.

Problem

"Changes in extreme weather will result in climate-related expenses totalling $13 billion by 2030", according to the Financial Accountability Office (FAO) (Canadian Press, 2022). Long-term, if global emissions peak by mid-century, climate hazards will increase infrastructure costs by $2.2 billion per year on average, without any climate adaptation, while if emissions continue to rise after 2050, those costs will rise by $4.1 billion per year on average, according to the report (Canadian Press, 2022). Between now and 2100, adaptation would contribute between $1.4 billion and $2.9 billion each year (Canadian Press, 2022). "While these additional climate-related expenses are significant, they are less costly for provincial and municipal governments in the long run than not adapting," the FAO noted (Canadian Press, 2022). Sea level rise, strong rains, and excessive temperatures are causing damage to infrastructure, and the harm is expected to worsen as climate change continues (UNEP, 2021). Flooding along rivers, lakes, and cities is exceeding the boundaries of flood prevention systems planned for historical conditions due to severe downpours, protracted rains, and rapid melting of the snowpack (UNEP, 2021). Moreover, the extreme heat is causing damage to transportation infrastructures like roads, rail lines, and airport runways.

Inger Andersen, Executive Director of UNEP stated, "As we seek to bridge the infrastructure gap and improve the quality of life of people everywhere, it is critical that we invest in sustainable infrastructure that adapts to future uncertain climate conditions; contributes to the decarbonization of the economy; protects biodiversity and minimizes pollution. Sustainable infrastructure is the only way we can ensure that people, nature and the environment thrive together" (UNEP, 2021). Unpredictable weather caused by climate change means more severe and frequent storms, which raises the risk of flooding because existing grey infrastructure systems (sewers, pumps, etc.) are ill-equipped to deal with more rainwater and runoff (GIO, 2021). Moreover, Cities have large sections of pavement and concrete buildings that absorb and retain heat, resulting in even higher air temperatures that exacerbate negative health effects and raise the energy costs required to cool buildings (GIO, 2021). To combat climate change, governments must drastically rethink infrastructure planning, delivery, and management to make it fit for a low-emission and resilient future (UNEP, 2021). Professor Jim Hall, Professor of Climate and Environmental Risk at the University of Oxford stated, "The central question is not whether we need infrastructure, but how it can be provided in ways that are sustainable, resilient and compatible with a net zero future. There is no simple answer to the question of how to provide climate-compatible infrastructure. It requires a myriad of choices, from the moment an infrastructure project is first conceived, to the end of its life when it is decommissioned or repurposed" (UNEP, 2021).

To combat climate change, governments must drastically rethink infrastructure planning, delivery, and management to make it fit for a low-emission and resilient future (UNEP, 2021).

Buildings and public infrastructure systems in Canada (such as bridges, highways, water and wastewater systems, energy transmission, and transit) are governed by rules and standards mostly based on historical climate data (Canada, 2022). In many cases, this has resulted in assets that were not meant to resist the present extreme weather occurrences, let alone the long-term effects of climate change (Canada, 2022). The increased likelihood of building and infrastructure collapse, as well as the accompanying threats to Canadians' well-being, necessitates a greater need to adapt and build resilience (Canada, 2022).

Climate-related risks such as floods, wildfires, droughts, and extreme weather events must be properly prepared for in our infrastructure and communities, particularly in Indigenous, northern, coastal, and rural regions (Canada, 2022). Investing in traditional and natural infrastructure solutions, such as retrofits and upgrades, can assist communities in building resilience, reducing disaster risks, and saving money in the long run (Canada, 2022).

Solutions

One way to help infrastructure and climate is to adopt green infrastructure. Green infrastructure can assist communities in addressing these issues. Green infrastructure is a tool that can help communities become more resilient to climate change. It extends from major urban areas to rural locations and contains both natural and man-made features. All of the system's components are valuable assets to our communities, but they lack consistent financing and policy support from higher levels of government (GIO, 2021). Green infrastructure is also a useful investment for governments because it can adapt to a variety of conditions that may arise as a result of the uncertainties around the effects of climate change (GIO, 2021). In New York City, Green Infrastructure describes an array of practices that use or mimic natural systems to manage stormwater runoff (NYC, n.d.). Green construction initiatives frequently concentrate on the structural building itself, and they frequently include programs relating to energy efficiency, building materials, structural water use reduction, and interior systems (e.g., heating, cooling, and lighting).

Green infrastructure techniques are complementary approaches that can be included in building envelopes through green roofs and green walls, but can also be extended beyond the building through integration into site design and typical infrastructure development (e.g., parking lots) (GIO, 2021). Green infrastructure practices can be less expensive than standard approaches in lot-level construction and design—depending on the scale and methodology, green infrastructure has been found to reduce project delivery costs, long-term maintenance expenses, and/or overall life-cycle costs (GIO, 2021). Furthermore, projects that incorporate green infrastructure principles into the planning and design phases are better positioned to capitalize on the cost savings, climate change resilience, and other advantages that green infrastructure practices provide (GIO, 2021). Green infrastructure intercepts absorb, and retains stormwater, reducing the amount of runoff that enters sewers during heavy rains. Living green infrastructure helps sustain infiltration to aquifers, recharge groundwater reserves, and maintain base flow in rivers by absorbing rain where it falls, relieving stress on local water supplies and lowering the need to import potable water. to the rest of the world, at the end of the world, at the end of the world, at the end of the world (GIO, 2021).

Green infrastructure reduces air temperatures by providing shade and evapotranspiration, so countering the urban heat island effect and its environmental and health consequences. It also decreases water thermal pollution by cooling stormwater before it enters naturally cool waterbodies through the filtering process (GIO, 2021). When less rainwater enters sewer systems, communities reduce their pumping and treatment demand, resulting in energy savings. Living green infrastructure reduces building energy demands for air conditioning and cooling in the summer by lowering temperatures and shading buildings and surrounding surfaces (GIO, 2021). This also produces pleasant microclimates that encourage walking and cycling, resulting in decreased vehicle use and greenhouse gas emissions (GIO, 2021).

Ways to Adopt Green Infrastructure:

Rain gardens: commonly defined as planted spaces that collect rainfall. Rain gardens are planted spaces on the sidewalk that are designed to collect and manage rainfall. Rain gardens are vegetated or landscaped depressions with an artificial soil covering that promote rainwater runoff infiltration into the underlying soil (NYC, n.d.). Rainwater, also known as "stormwater runoff," travels down the street gutter, along the curb, and into the rain garden when it rains. In a process known as "infiltration," rainfall is absorbed by the sandy soil on top (engineered soil) and the stone layer at the bottom and seeps into the earth beneath (NYC, n.d.). Some of the water will be absorbed by the trees and plants as a result of evapotranspiration, and any residual water will evaporate when the rain event has ended (NYC, n.d.). During a strong rainstorm, stormwater flows into the rain garden, but some water may bypass the inlet and enter the catch basin directly. If the rain garden fills up, the stormwater will overflow at the exit and pour into the catch basin as usual (NYC, n.d.).

Permeable paving: refers to a variety of materials and processes, such as permeable pavers or porous concrete, that allow water to soak through the paving and sink into the ground. Permeable paving can be utilized in place of impermeable concrete or asphalt (NYC, 2021).

Urban forests: trees and shrubs growing in urban and suburban settings, including those on roadways, parking lots, private property, and parks and natural areas, comprise urban forests (TRCACA, n.d.). Large trees, in particular, maximize the advantages of this form of green infrastructure. A 75-cm diameter tree, for example, intercepts ten times more air pollution and can store up to 90 times more carbon than a 15-cm diameter tree in Toronto (TRCACA, n.d.). Carbon is reduced by 3-7% for every 10% increase in the urban tree canopy (GreenBlue Urban, 2022).

Bioswales: linear, planted channels that allow stormwater to be collected, transported, filtered, and absorbed (TRCACA, n.d.). Bioswales collect rainwater runoff from neighbouring paved surfaces and hold it long enough for it to slowly sink into the deep soil and maybe rock drainage layer. Bioswales, as opposed to ditches, delay and filter stormwater before it enters the stormwater pipe system (TRCACA, n.d.).

Green roofs: employ vegetated roof covers that contain growing material and plants. In vertical gardens, green walls comprise specific modular parts fastened to building walls (TRCACA, n.d.).

These are only a few examples of green infrastructures that can be implemented in cities to aid in climate change mitigation and urban improvement (TRCACA, n.d.). Green infrastructure has the potential to cut hard infrastructure construction costs, maintain ageing infrastructure, and stimulate economic development (TRCACA, n.d.). Furthermore, it can aid in the reduction of energy consumption and prices, the reduction of hard infrastructure life cycle costs, and the rise of carbon storage and sequestration (TRCACA, n.d.). A single mature tree may absorb 21.6kg of carbon each year. Increased canopy cover aids in the reduction of air pollution, with street trees lowering particulate matter concentrations by 15-20% (GreenBlue Urban, 2022).

It also benefits people because Tree-lined properties sell faster and are valued 5% to 15% more than those without trees (GreenBlue Urban, 2022). Furthermore, properly positioned windbreak trees surrounding buildings can save up to 25% on winter heating expenditures (GreenBlue Urban, 2022).

In addition to green infrastructure, there is grey and blue infrastructure. Dams, seawalls, highways, pipes, and water treatment plants are examples of grey infrastructure. This is a classic human-engineered technique for water management, such as pipelines and hard surfaces. The goal is to build a network of water retention and purification infrastructure to limit the flow of stormwater during rain events, preventing flooding and reducing the number of pollutants entering waterways (Conservation.org, 2022). However, adjusting to the rising effects of climate breakdown, particularly for coastlines facing sea-level rise and greater storms, necessitates a shift in our infrastructure (Conservation.org, 2022).

Blue infrastructure refers to urban water infrastructure such as ponds, lakes, streams, and rivers, as well as stormwater provision. Sustainable drainage schemes are normally classified under this category, but they are also occasionally referred to as green infrastructure (GreenBlue Urban, 2022). The advantages of blue infrastructure include the ability of potential attenuation area inside specialized soil to hold 22%-35% water by soil volume without affecting tree health and the stormwater runoff is reduced by 2% for every 5% increase in tree canopy cover (GreenBlue Urban, 2022). Moreover, arborFlow SuDS can filter up to 95% of contaminants from stormwater runoff, including microplastics, hydrocarbons, and metals (GreenBlue Urban, 2022). Healthy urban trees can hold massive amounts of water on their canopy and branch structure, up to 70% of the first hour of a rain event (GreenBlue Urban, 2022).

Combining Methods

Grey and blue infrastructure can be coupled with green infrastructure to improve both the climate and our infrastructure. A Green-gray infrastructure, for example, combines nature protection and restoration (including natural coastal buffers such as mangroves and seagrasses) with conventional measures (such as concrete dams and seawalls). As a result, communities are fortified against climate change while also receiving fresh water, clean air, coastal protection, and other natural benefits (Conservation.org, 2022). According to research produced by Charles j Vörösmarty et al., sustainable development necessitates dependable water resources, yet traditional water management has mostly failed to avert environmental damage and contain infrastructure costs. The article investigates the global viability of integrating natural capital with engineering-based (green-gray) techniques to address water security issues in the twenty-first century (Vörösmarty et al, 2021). Recent studies on human water security suggest that population and economic expansion, mismanaged water usage, climate extremes, and a general failure to effectively conserve landscapes and inland waterways pose serious worldwide challenges (Vörösmarty et al, 2021). Traditional engineering, with centralized water treatment and distribution systems and abundant, often huge river impoundments and flood control structures, has been the dominant approach to these difficulties (Vörösmarty et al, 2021). With many successful "worked examples" such as wetlands functioning alongside massive flood control infrastructure, healthy catchments purifying urban water supplies, and wetlands providing effluent treatment in urban water systems, well-designed combinations of natural capital and built infrastructure can boost the performance and reduce the costs of engineered solutions.

Blended systems could thus play a major role in future HWS, but only in places with considerable natural capital endowments. To protect such potential, comprehensive stewardship of ecosystem services, incorporating regional if not continental-scale perspectives, will be required (Vörösmarty et al, 2021). Cost-cutting and long-term water resource development can be accomplished by maintaining natural capital and wisely incorporating it into the next generation of water management systems. An improved collaboration between natural capital and traditionally-engineered infrastructure researchers and practitioners, beginning with training our next-generation workforce to co-manage issues that go far beyond engineering alone (e.g., social and environmental equity), should go a long way toward achieving these goals (Vörösmarty et al, 2021). As a result, society will benefit from the non-economic value of sustainably managed natural capital, such as biodiversity, and important earth system support services such as climate stabilization. Traditional engineering is an important component of the solution, but it is neither economically nor environmentally viable as the primary method of sustainable water development.

Combining Blue and Green infrastructure (BGI) is an efficient approach offering a sustainable natural solution to urban and climatic difficulties in this scenario. Vegetation aids in the elimination of air pollution, stormwater management, and heat island effects, as well as the creation of more pleasant and less stressful living environments (GreenBlue Urban, 2022). By combining water management and green infrastructure, blue-green strives to restore the naturally oriented water cycle while also adding to amenities (GreenBlue Urban, 2022).

According to a publication by Lamond and Everett, BGI's sustainable functioning and benefit provision are dependent on the behaviour of individuals who use it, hence local stewardship is frequently advocated to promote maintenance. BGI has been argued to provide numerous additional benefits, including improved air and water quality, aesthetics, biodiversity, and amenity. As a result, it is increasingly viewed as a viable means of mitigating flood risk while also improving the public realm on a global scale. BGI cannot be simply a national, regional, or local government initiative; it must involve the local public in new stewardship practices to be sustainable (Lamond & Everett, 2019). To achieve behavioural changes, communities must be engaged, which is generally accomplished through the communication of prospective advantages to urge communities to realize and respect the BGI. BGI is a viable, cost-effective, and important option for metropolitan areas confronting climate change challenges (Lamond & Everett, 2019).

The blue-green systems aid in the removal of contaminants from water and air, the reduction of rainwater into the pipe system, and the increase of managed impermeable area that treats urban runoff (Vancouver, 2022). Furthermore, it can aid in increasing total green area that treatments urban runoff and mitigating the urban heat island effect (Vancouver, 2022).

A significant feature of BGI is its multifunctionality, or the capacity to perform multiple functions and give multiple benefits within the same geographical space. This means that BGI uses the interrelationships between plants and the water cycle to improve urban living conditions (Brears, 2018). As a result, both sustainable development and water- and greenery-related ecosystem services benefit. A green roof, for example, can reduce stormwater runoff and water pollution while simultaneously reducing the urban heat island effect, boosting building insulation, and providing habitat for wildlife (Brears, 2018). It should be noted that not all green places or environmental elements are BGI. They must not only be of excellent quality, but they must also be a part of an integrated BGI network and provide many benefits (Brears, 2018). For example, an urban park may be considered a BGI component if, in addition to absorbing excess water runoff, it provides recreational activities and benefits wildlife (Brears, 2018).

Conclusion

Overall people will be able to minimize urban heat, lessen building energy demands, restore groundwater reservoirs, and so on with green, grey, blue, and green-blue infrastructure. Green infrastructure systems built throughout a town, city, or across a regional watershed can deliver cleaner air and water, as well as significant value to the community in the form of flood protection, diverse habitats, and beautiful green places. BGI can be built at many spatial sizes. BGI is vital not just for managing excess water but also for replenishing valuable water supplies (Brears, 2018). Grants, fast-tracking applications, and educating the public on the benefits of BGI are some of the fiscal and non-financial measures that can be utilized to increase BGI adoption (Brears, 2018). Moreover, not only can these infrastructures bring cross-sectoral advantages and serve as a foundation for changes in social and environmental dimensions, but also economically. Infrastructure investments will boost the economy by producing new jobs, new sources of revenue, trade opportunities, and assets and services. The best use of local labour and materials can also help to improve the local economy and reduce poverty. The methods for implementing these innovations and their benefits will undoubtedly enhance both our future lives and the environment.

References

Brears, R. (2018, December 25). The role of blue-green infrastructure in managing urban water resources. Retrieved from https://medium.com/mark-and-focus/the-role-of-blue-green-infrastructure-in-managing-urban-water-resources-dd058007ba1a

Canada, I. (2022, June 23). Government of Canada. Retrieved from https://www.infrastructure.gc.ca/plan/crbcpi-irccipb-eng.html

Charles J. Vörösmarty et al. Global Environmental Change. (2021, September 04). A green-gray path to Global Water Security and sustainable infrastructure. Retrieved https://www.sciencedirect.com/science/article/pii/S0959378021001230

Conservation.org. Green-Gray Infrastructure. (2022). Retrieved from https://www.conservation.org/projects/green-gray-infrastructure

GreenBlue Urban. Why use green & blue infrastructure? (2022, December 06). Retrieved from https://greenblue.com/gb/about-us/why-green-and-blue/#:~:text=Blue%20infrastructure%20usually%20relates%20to,also%20labelled%20as%20green%20infrastructure.

Green Infrastructure Ontario (GIO). Climate change. (2021, January 29). Retrieved from https://greeninfrastructureontario.org/climate-change/

Introduction to green infrastructure - amazon web services. (n.d.). Retrieved from https://trcaca.s3.ca-central-1.amazonaws.com/app/uploads/2016/08/17163548/Introduction-to-Green-Infrastructure_uploaded-June-2018.pdf

Jessica Lamond, Glyn Everett. Landscape and Urban Planning. (2019, August 27). Sustainable Blue-green infrastructure: A social practice approach to understanding community preferences and stewardship. Retrieved from https://www.sciencedirect.com/science/article/pii/S0169204618309770

New report reveals how infrastructure defines our climate. (2021, October 12). Retrieved from https://www.unep.org/news-and-stories/press-release/new-report-reveals-how-infrastructure-defines-our-climate#:~:text=The%20findings%20highlight%20that%20infrastructure,and%20the%20Sustainable%20Development%20Goals.

The Canadian Press. Climate change effect on public transportation infrastructure to cost billions: FAO - constructconnect.com. (2022, September 23). Retrieved from https://canada.constructconnect.com/dcn/news/infrastructure/2022/09/climate-change-effect-on-public-transportation-infrastructure-to-cost-billions-fao

Types of green infrastructure. (n.d.). Retrieved from https://www.nyc.gov/site/dep/water/types-of-green-infrastructure.page

Vancouver, C. (2022). Blue Green Systems. Retrieved from https://vancouver.ca/home-property-development/blue-green-systems.aspx

Chapter 5

Insect Food Harvesting

Jannat Irfan

Climate change and food?

Earth's climate has been changing drastically over the past decades. Human activities have resulted in the release of increasing quantities of carbon dioxide and other greenhouse gases, thus contributing to global climate change by additional heating of the atmosphere (Bein et al., 2019). The world has warmed up by 1.1 degrees Celsius compared to last century (Bein et al., 2019). The warming up of the earth not only affects climate change but food as well. However, food production and manufacturing are also one of the factors that caused the earth's temperature to rise. Both the food industry and climate change impact one another negatively. There is a strong relationship between the food industry and climate change that must be studied deeply by professionals to spread awareness and save the earth from further damage.

Climate change impacts food production

Climate change impacts food production negatively. Climate change disrupts food availability, reduces access to food, and affects food quality (US EPA, n.d.). For example, a projected increase in temperatures, changes in precipitation patterns, changes in extreme weather events, and reductions in water availability result in low agricultural productivity (US EPA, n.d.). When there is low agricultural productivity then the prices in the market increase for the few high-productivity items, which can lead to food insecurity in many individuals. Food insecurity can lead to malnutrition and various diseases. Moreover, any climate-related disturbance to food distribution and transport, domestically and internationally, has significant impacts on not only the safety and quality of food but also food access which can also lead to food insecurity (US EPA, n.d.). Impacts on the global food supply concern all countries on earth because food shortages can cause humanitarian crises and national security concerns (US EPA, n.d.).

Food production impact on climate change

Food production, manufacturing, and transportation are a few of the factors that contribute to unhealthy climate change. Farming requires a lot of pesticide and fertiliser use. Artificial fertilisers and pesticides are unsustainable because they are energy intensive to produce and thus are dependent on cheap fossil fuels to be made (Maple Ridge, British Columbia, n.d.). Also, as we know, fossil fuels emit greenhouse gases, and the production of artificial fertilisers and pesticides contributes to climate change, becoming a major factor for the long-term sustainability of food production (Maple Ridge, British Columbia, n.d.). These chemicals can cause soil to lose its fertility which can damage the soil's capability of growing trees which contributes to a healthy environment. Moreover, fossil fuels are also used to fuel farm equipment used in conventional agriculture, such as trucks, tractors, graders, etc. This equipment can cause air pollution which contributes to climate change and can impact the health of individuals as well such as farmers and food industry workers (Maple Ridge, British Columbia, n.d.).

Farming also contributes to climate change negatively through the release of methane which is one of the major greenhouse gases. Methane is produced from livestock animals that are used for farming (Maple Ridge, British Columbia, n.d.). When livestock animals such as cows, goats, sheep, and buffalos eat plants to survive, their digestive systems produce methane gas which is excreted as waste into the environment (Maple Ridge British Columbia, n.d.). Methane is present in the air in high amounts because with the growing population of human beings on Earth, farming land and need is increased too which requires the need to have more livestock animals too and when all the livestock animals consume food, they produce a huge amount of solid waste and methane (Maple Ridge, British Columbia, n.d.).

In addition, the climate change damage to food production is not only limited to farming chemicals, farming, and livestock animals, it is also caused by deforestation (Maple Ridge, British Columbia, n.d.). Harvesting and producing crops requires a huge amount of nutrients, water, and energy that is taken away from the land (Maple Ridge, British Columbia, n.d.). Moreover, to raise crops, large tracts of land are needed. Moreover, developing farmland requires that deforestation take place. This leaves the land and the soil barren and unfriendly for the growth and development of new and old organisms and their ecosystems (Maple Ridge, British Columbia, n.d.).

As mentioned above, transportation is a factor that contributes to climate change as well. Transportation of food items from farms to markets locally and internationally influences the unsustainability of the food production systems (Maple Ridge, British Columbia, n.d.). Vehicles require a lot of fossil fuels which cause air pollution and cause the climate to be impacted negatively.

Lastly, another way in which food impacts climate change negatively is through food waste. After the food has been grown and transported and prepared for consumption, it harms the environment by throwing away the leftovers (Maple Ridge, British Columbia, n.d.). Food is wasted throughout the entire production chain too, not only after humans have consumed it. For example, from the initial crop growth to the supermarket screening, to the final household consumption food is wasted (Maple Ridge, British Columbia, n.d.). In Canada, 40% of food is wasted at the retail level due to the food not meeting the high cosmetic standard. And Canadians waste $31 billion of food every year. This causes 3.3 billion tons of carbon dioxide, which is a greenhouse gas that contributes to climate change (Maple Ridge, British Columbia, n.d.).

Can climate change be reversed?

Climate change, unfortunately, cannot be reversed. However, it can be prevented from changing further. Many countries and their citizens have been putting in a great amount of effort to make sustainable changes to how food is produced so that it affects climate less. For example, synthetic products that can be made in the lab are being produced and through this conservation method, no big farmlands with livestock will be required. Moreover, various donation programs cause less food to be wasted. In addition, an interesting and highly debated method that can help reduce the negative impact of food systems on climate change is the insect protein alternative to animal meat and vegetables. This chapter will be talking about insect food harvesting and its relation to climate change.

How are insects harvested and how does the process impact the climate?

The United Nations (UN), global sustainable development agenda called "Transforming our world: The 2030 agenda for sustainable development" adopted 17 sustainable goals (Moruzzo et al., 2021). The purpose of these 17 sustainable development goals is to stimulate action over the next decade in areas of critical importance for humanity and the planet (Moruzzo et al., 2021). According to the FAO, food production will have to increase by 70% to feed the world's population by 2050 (70. This population growth will undoubtedly have a huge effect on climate change as more population means more consumption and changes in consumption patterns, such as demanding higher animal protein (Moruzzo et al., 2021). This causes concern for the current population as a lot of deforestation has already been done. The soil is drastically changing which puts a lot of pressure on the current and future limited resources (Moruzzo et al., 2021). Moreover, this causes competition for land to produce food, feed, and fuel and makes challenges for environmental sustainability even more difficult (Moruzzo et al., 2021). Moreover, one-third of food is wasted, 25.9% of the Earth's population is suffering from both moderate and severe levels of food insecurity since 2019 and this is increasing, and 8.9% of the Earth's population is estimated to have been undernourished (Moruzzo et al., 2021).

One of the alternatives to all the issues mentioned above is insect food harvesting. Insect food harvesting is the practice of raising and breeding insects as livestock instead of animals such as cows. These insects are called mini-livestock or micro-livestock (Wikimedia Foundation, 2022). This idea of insect harvesting arises because insects are the most abundant animals in the world, with all species accounting for more than 70% of the global animal population (Wikimedia Foundation, 2022). Moreover, insect food harvesting does not require as much energy as conventional farming. Furthermore, insect food harvesting causes less damage to the environment thus causing fewer changes to the climate. Edible insects have economic, nutritional, and ecological advantages, their production deserves more attention from both governments and assistance programmes to ensure food security (Wikimedia Foundation, 2022).

Insects also are rich in proteins, and fats, and have amino acids and fatty acid profiles that are well-balanced for human beings to intake (Moruzzo et al., 2021). Furthermore, compared to conventional livestock, insect production has a lower environmental impact because it requires limited land and water which leads to reduced amounts of greenhouse gases and carbon dioxide emissions (Moruzzo et al., 2021). Moreover, insects have a high feed conversion rate which means that they require less food to produce the same amount of animal proteins compared to conventional animals such as cows or goats (Moruzzo et al., 2021). In addition, insects can also be cultured or produced on locally available industrial and agricultural waste streams which is beneficial for the climate and the environment. Insects can be gathered and collected from nature or they can be farmed via simple techniques and minimal facilities requiring minimal land or capital and have a quick growth rate (Moruzzo et al., 2021).

There is potential for insect protein to replace animal meat as a source of human diets because of climate changes and the rapid advancement in the food industry and individuals leaning towards more sustainable options. Especially in western societies, edible insects have a greater potential as animal feed than as human food because of cultural biases associated with harmful insects, although abundant characteristics of edible insects should benefit human health (Kim et al., 2019). As mentioned above, using insects as a major protein source can potentially solve major problems related to the conventional food supply chain, which includes global water, land, climate change, and energy deficits (Kim et al., 2019).

Moving onto how insect harvesting can contribute to the United nation's sustainable development goals, it is a known fact that livestock contributes drastically to global greenhouse gas emissions, however, insect harvesting produces low amounts of greenhouse gases and ammonia (Moruzzo et al., 2021). Insect harvesting supports sustainable development goal 13: "Take urgent action to combat climate change and its impacts". Four insect species were reported by the United Nations that can be used for food harvesting and produce less greenhouse gas emissions than ruminants and pigs (Moruzzo et al., 2021). Also, ammonia levels of insect farming are lower than conventional livestock animals (Moruzzo et al., 2021). Insects can become resilient mini-livestock production in countries that are currently facing the effects of extreme climate changes (Moruzzo et al., 2021). Moreover, the low needed amount of water for insect harvesting, the capability to be reared on the side streams, and the ability to grow in extreme weather climates such as very hot or very cold can all be ensured by insect harvesting or insect farming (Moruzzo et al., 2021).

Insect harvesting also supports the United Nations sustainable development goal 15: "Protect, restore and promote sustainable use of terrestrial ecosystems, sustainability manages forests, combat desertification, and halt and reverse land degradation and halt biodiversity loss". Insect harvesting contributes to mitigating biodiversity reduction in two ways; firstly, through insect rearing and secondly through insects being food for other livestock animals (Moruzzo et al., 2021). Insect rearing does not require direct contact with the ground and the soil, and it can be done in any environment (Moruzzo et al., 2021). This reduces land use and helps in restoring the ecosystem. Insects can be fed to conventional livestock which can help in reducing plant production for feed and contribute to increased biodiversity and combating desertification (Moruzzo et al., 2021).

Insect harvesting also supports the United Nations' sustainable development goal 6: "Ensure availability and sustainable management of water and sanitation for all". Insects are capable of contributing to improved water sanitation when they are directly reared on human or animal faecal matter (Moruzzo et al., 2021). Some insects such as flies already use faeces as their main nutritional resource for producing offspring and developing their larval and adult stages (Moruzzo et al., 2021). Insects using faeces as a substrate helps to reduce all kinds of pollution in the environment and insects that are reared on such substrates can be used as feed as well for the production and energy of human beings and livestock animals (Moruzzo et al., 2021).

Lastly, insect harvesting also supports the United Nations' sustainable development goal 2: "End Hunger, achieve food security, and improve nutrition and promote sustainable agriculture". Using insects as a source of protein can reduce human beings' dependence on the feed gained from conventional farming, which causes climate damage and causes food security because of price issues and accessibility issues (Moruzzo et al., 2021). Through culturing insects on local waste streams, any leftovers can be used as biofertilizers which can help farmers in using fewer chemical-based fertilisers (Moruzzo et al., 2021). Insects are highly edible foods and approved by doctors as well and present no harm to human health. Insects are healthy and sustainable food and feed alternatives that can help resolve many issues such as hunger. Insects can be produced at a faster rate than conventional food and can be produced anywhere in the world which resolves the issues related to accessibility hence it resolves some aspects of food insecurity.

Are insects a viable alternative to conventional animal-based and plant-based food?

The EuroNews posted an article about Danish Crown Prince Frederick attending a Citizens Sustainability Summit and sampling a cookie made partly out of the insect cricket proteins (Symons & Sen, 2021). Moreover, Bloomberg News recently reported that a company called NTG Holdings received $20 million in investments to develop animal feed from the black soldier fly maggots (Sguazzin, 2022). This presents that insect as a protein is making their way up to take over conventional animal-based and plant-based food.

Of course, some individuals might not be comfortable with consuming insects however, insect harvesting has health benefits as well as environmental benefits which makes it a great source of protein for human beings as well as other animals. Individuals do not need to consume insects alone. There are many ways in which insects can be incorporated into the human diet. González et al (2019) studied the potential use of flour made from insects as an additive in commercial bread making. Their goal was to assess the impact of three types of insect flour on dough behaviour and bread quality (González et al., 2019). From commercial insect producers and farmers, four types of insect species were bought for this study. The insects were then frozen, freeze-dried under vacuum conditions, and milled into powder of comparable weight to commercial wheat flour (González et al., 2019). The nutritional quality was assessed for both insect and wheat flour. Then the commercial bread recipes were altered by replacing 5% of the wheat flour with insect flour. Then after the flour was baked it was assessed for nutritional quality, texture, shape, and taste. The baked product made out of insect flour was reported to show a better nutrition profile when compared to wheat flour (González et al., 2019). The insect flour had higher protein and fat count and lower carbohydrate count which means that the insect flour is healthier (González et al., 2019). There were significant differences in nutrient profiles between the four types of insect species. Moreover, doughs made from insect flour fermented and rose better than wheat flour dough. The final, baked loaves were similar in appearance. In essence, this study showed that insects can be used as flour as well and there are many other possibilities as well where insects can be used in daily food products. This study also showed that insects do contain a better nutritional value than conventional foods such as wheat (González et al., 2019).

Moreover, a study done by Han et al (2016) showed that insects are safe to consume. In their study, yellow mealworm larva was fed to rats and a toxicology assessment was performed on the rats which included mortality, clinical signs, body and organ weights, food consumption, ophthalmology, urinalysis, hematology, serum chemistry, gross findings, histopathologic examination, and allergic reactions (Han et al., 2016). The results of the toxicology assessment found no health-related issues in the rats and the study concluded that it is safe to consume yellow mealworm however further research is needed (Han et al., 2016).

Conclusion

Through analyzing the studies mentioned above, insect-based protein has the potential to form part of the future human food systems. Insect harvesting contains the capability to mimic the same nutritional values as conventional food which comes from farming and livestock. In essence, insect harvesting is a great alternative to animal and plant-based farming which causes high rates of global greenhouse gas emissions which causes the climate to drastically change. Insect harvesting also supports the United Nations Sustainable development goals. It is important for individuals around all counties as well to choose healthier options when it comes to their food because food affects climate change and the environment of our earth. Hence, it is our responsibility to spread awareness and choose better alternatives, such as insect food harvesting to save the Earth. If insect harvesting does take over animal-based food and plant-based food in the next decade, then this will be a huge benefit for the current climate condition. Moreover, to change the climate, all individuals need to take recycling food waste and leftovers seriously as well. Big corporations in the food chain industry should also develop programs that support the United Nations' sustainable goals and promote awareness as well. Moreover, in schools and colleges, it should be taught to students how food production takes place and what are its effects on the climate and the Earth so that more awareness is spread. Climate can only be changed if all countries and individuals living in it work together for the betterment of Earth and a safer future.

References

Bein, T., Karagiannidis, C., & Quintel, M. (2019). Climate change, global warming, and Intensive Care. Intensive Care Medicine, 46(3), 485–487. doi: 10.1007/s00134-019-05888-4

US EPA. (n.d.) Climate Impacts on Agriculture and Food Supply | Climate Change Impacts. Retrieved from https://climatechange. chicago.gov/climate-impacts/climate-impacts-agriculture-and-food-supply#:~:text=Climate%20change%20can%20disrupt%20 food,result%20in%20reduced%20agricultural%20productivity

Maple Ridge British Columbia. (n.d.). Environmental impacts of food production. 2020_Horizontal_FullColour. Retrieved from https://www.mapleridge.ca/1776/Food-Production#:~:text=Farming%20also%20contributes%20to%20 climate,is%20excreted%20as%20gaseous%20waste

Wikimedia Foundation. (2022). Insect farming. Wikipedia. Retrieved from https://en.wikipedia.org/wiki/Insect_farming

Symons A, Sen M. (2021). Danish royal eats cricket cookie: here's why insect-based food is growing in popularity. Euronews.green Sept 21. Retrieved from https://www.euronews.com/green/2022/09/21/ danish-royal-eats-cricket-cookie-heres-why-insect-based-food-is-growing-in-popularity

Kim, T.-K., Yong, H. I., Kim, Y.-B., Kim, H.-W., & Choi, Y.-S. (2019). Edible insects as a protein source: A review of public perception, processing technology, and research trends. Food Science of Animal Resources, 39(4), 521–540. doi: 10.5851/kosfa.2019.e53

Moruzzo, R., Mancini, S., & Guidi, A. (2021). Edible insects and sustainable development goals. Insects, 12(6), 557. doi: 10.3390/insects12060557

Sguazzin A. (2022). Insect protein company gets $20 million from Sumitomo, ING, and Mandala. Bloomberg News, Sept 19. Retrieved from https://www.bnnbloomberg.ca/insect-protein-company-gets-20-million-funding-from-sumitomo-ing-and-mandala-1.1820596

González CM, Garzón R, Rosell CM. (2019). Insects as ingredients for bakery goods. A comparison study of H. illucens, A. domestica, and T. molitor flours. Innovative Food Science and Emerging Technologies 51(1), 205-210.

Han, S.-R., Lee, B.-S., Jung, K.-J., Yu, H.-J., Yun, E.-Y., Hwang, J. S., & Moon, K.-S. (2016). Safety assessment of freeze-dried powdered tenebrio molitor larvae (yellow mealworm) as Novel Food Source: Evaluation of 90-day toxicity in Sprague-Dawley rats. Regulatory Toxicology and Pharmacology, 77, 206–212. doi: 10.1016/j.yrtph.2016.03.006

Chapter 6

Application of Solar Energy in regards to Climate Change

Syed Rizvi

Introduction

Throughout many eras, Earth has undergone many transformations and changes; from the Pleistocene Ice Age to the changes in the tectonic plates. Therefore, what makes climate change different and a huge area of concern? It is concerning because it is mainly caused by human activity and is preventable. Researchers are attempting to incorporate many forms of renewable energy to sustain societal needs, fortunately, one of the methods seems promising - solar energy. Sunlight is free, abundant, and accessible almost everywhere. Sun emits solar energy at a rate of 3.8 x 1023 kW, from which 1.8 x 1023 kW is received by Earth (Kannan & Vakeesan, 2016). However, solar energy is hard to implement due to the development of a country, poor technological advancement, socioeconomic status of people, and politico-economic climate. Energy demands and consumption are exponentially increasing as our population has increased by approximately two billion in a single generation (Kannan & Vakeesan, 2016). Furthermore, with the increase in technological and economic development, humans require greater consumption of energy (Timilsina, Kurdgelashvili, & Narbel, 2012). There is an urgent need for sustainable renewable energy as energy industries are polluting the Earth and destroying ecosystems by burning fossil fuels. Therefore, this chapter will focus on the different applications of solar energy and its impact on climate change.

What is solar energy

Solar Energy is characterized by different categories; passive and active, thermal and photovoltaic, and concentrating and non-concentrating (Timilsina et al., 2012). Solar technology that collects energy without converting heat or light from the sun into other forms of energy is referred to as passive. A person keeping all their windows closed during winter, or the use of daylight savings are all examples of passive solar energy. However, active solar energy technology is further divided into two groups; photovoltaic (PV) and thermal. Photovoltaic technology converts "radiant energy contained in light quanta into electrical energy when light falls upon a semiconductor material, causing electron excitation and strongly enhancing conductivity" (Timilsina et al., 2012). The use of solar radiation in electricity was first observed by Bacquerel in 1839 (Sampaio & González, 2017). The process of photovoltaic effect occurs when two energy bands are present in a semiconductor. One band is required to have a presence of electrons, known as the valence band, whereas the second band, or the conduction band, is to have no presence of electrons (Sampaio & González, 2017). The material of semiconductors is commonly made from Silicon, which is, fortunately, the second most abundant element on Earth - oxygen being the first. Photovoltaic technology is currently available in a crystalline silicon-based cell and a thin film made from different semiconductor materials, "including amorphous silicon, cadmium–telluride and copper indium gallium diselenide" (Timilsina et al., 2012). Silicon cells are the most popular due to their abundance, but also the fact that it is a stable and non-toxic element, and has a bandgap of 1.12 eV, which is approximately identical to the solar spectrum. Lastly, silicon as an element is easily compatible with microelectronics that have silicon-based parts such as transistors and some circuits (Sampaio & González, 2017). Moreover, the photovoltaic effect occurs when sunlight allows for the outermost electron to move from the valence band to the conduction band. With silicon, the electron needs 1.12 eV (electro-volts) to pass the gap. Almost all photovoltaic technologies include a PN junction, also known as photovoltaic cells or solar cells in the semiconductor, where the photo voltage is stored (Sampaio & González, 2017).

Aside from PV technology, we have thermal technology that comes in two forms; solar thermal non-electric and solar thermal electric (Timilsina et al., 2012). Solar non-electric refers to technologies that store and use solar heat, such as solar water heaters, cooling systems, solar cookers, etc. However, solar thermal electric energy, also known as concentrated solar power, uses solar heat to water and produce rising steam, which then turns the turbines for electricity (Timilsina et al., 2012). According to Kurokawa K, Komoto K, Vleuten VDP, and Faiman D, they estimate that PV cells distributed in 4% of the surface area of the world's deserts will produce enough electricity to match the demand of the world's consumption rate. Around 2016, engineers developed PV panels that operate at an efficiency rate of 90% after 10 years and 80% after 25 years, however, this rate has dramatically improved in the year 2022 (Kannan & Vakeesan, 2016). However, these rates are not always consistent due to the multiple environmental effects, not including solar intensity and solar flux. Thus, solar panels come with a device known as a tracker. Trackers are implemented by using one or two axes to keep PV photo thermal panels in a position perpendicular to solar radiation during daylight. (Kannan & Vakeesan, 2016). Therefore, several research projects are being conducted to obtain consistent and efficient solar energy without the huge fluctuation in storage. In places where solar energy is fluctuating, hybrid systems are built where PV systems are combined with other electrical systems, such as diesel-powered generators, wind turbines, hydro turbines, etc. (Kannan & Vakeesan, 2016). Furthermore, solar energy can be implemented in modern architecture, inside and outside.

Implementation and usage of solar energy

In 2022, 36% of CO_2 emissions and 40% of electrical usage were from HVAC; standing for Heating, Ventilation, and Air Conditioning (Castillo-González, Comino, Navas-Martos, & Ruiz de Adana, 2022). Therefore, experimental solar HVAC systems are introduced to reduce those figures in every household to tackle climate change. An experimental prototype was installed in Andaltec, Martos, Southern Spain, that consisted of a desiccant wheel-based system and a solar field. The prototype involved a desiccant wheel, evaporative cooling, a heating coil, and a small hydraulic pump to pump the water. To compare, a conventional direct expansion-based system is used. The HVAC system is designed to control air humidity and air temperature in space; thus, it involves an expansion unit to cool and dehumidify air (Castillo-González, Comino, Navas-Martos, & Ruiz de Adana, 2022). After the experiment, weak points in the experimental solar HVAC system were discovered. Firstly, the structure of the system weighed around 312. kg and the collector of the solar field weighed 55 kg, therefore, a weight reduction of more than 50% is achieved by replacing the steel with glass fiber-reinforced polypropylene. Secondly, the materials in the solar field are replaced from aluminum to steel because aluminum poses a higher carbon footprint in the manufacturing phase where an excessive amount of energy is required to convert bauxite into aluminum. Although steel is three times heavier than aluminum, it is also three times cheaper (Castillo-González, Comino, Navas-Martos, & Ruiz de Adana, 2022). Solar photovoltaic technology is expensive and complex and requires advanced technology to manufacture and install (Kannan & Vakeesan, 2016). Therefore, it is imperative to reduce the costs of solar HVAC systems to compete with the traditional systems we have. Furthermore, the desiccant wheel-based system carried out 100% of treated outside air, whereas the conventional direct expansion-based system ensured 30 - 40% of treated outside air. The experimental HVAC system ensured a higher indoor air quality supply, which is a great advantage against the conventional systems as "Americans, on average, spend approximately 90 percent of their time indoors where the concentrations of some pollutants are often 2 to 5 times higher than typical outdoor concentrations (Indoor Air Quality | US EPA, 2017). Upon the results of the experiment, it was deduced that the desiccant wheel-based system consumed a higher amount of material due to the change to steel, thus explaining, the higher values of ozone layer depletion, land used potential, carcinogenic effect potential, and respiratory effects potential indicators (Castillo-González, Comino, Navas-Martos, & Ruiz de Adana, 2022).

However, the desiccant wheel wheel-based system used a higher amount of material due to the use of steel, which explains the increased values. On the contrary, the direct expansion-based system contributed to a higher value of ecotoxicity potential and mineral depletion, since there was a higher consumption of copper and energy used as compared to the desiccant wheel-based system (Castillo-González, Comino, Navas-Martos, & Ruiz de Adana, 2022). The experimental prototype - the desiccant wheel-based system, "generates a lower impact in all categories, between 2% and 10% less than DX1 (direct expansion-based system)" (Castillo-González, Comino, Navas-Martos, & Ruiz de Adana, 2022). The highest and most significant difference between the experimental and conventional systems is their climate change potential. However, these figures are a comparison between the prototype and the conventional HVAC system. Using the new design which optimized the weight, size, and material needed and the material reusing strategy, a reduction of 60% in climate change potential as compared to a conventional HVAC is achieved. "A proper DW-based system weight optimisation strategy could lead to a 30%, 5%, and 20% reduction in environmental impact for the categories of human health, ecosystem quality, and resource consumption, respectively" (Castillo-González, Comino, Navas-Martos, & Ruiz de Adana, 2022).

Integrated Photovoltaic Systems

Approximately 40% of worldwide energy and 33% of global greenhouse gas emissions in both developed and developing countries come from buildings (Abdelrazik, Shboul, Elwardany, Zohny, & Osama, 2022). Therefore, it would make the most sense to put industrial and academic power into developing efficient and eco-friendly technology to combat that figure. Building integrated photovoltaic systems, or BIPVs, are a popular alternative, where arrays of photovoltaic (PV) panels are mounted on top of the roof, and sometimes the walls, of a building (Kannan & Vakeesan, 2016).

Building integrated photovoltaic/thermal (BIPV/T) systems couples the photovoltaic modules and a solar thermal system to generate both electrical and thermal energy (Abdelrazik, Shboul, Elwardany, Zohny, & Osama, 2022). The two systems merged in one can produce more energy per unit surface area, and reduce the cost of manufacturing and installation than the BIPVs and thermal system working as two. BIPV/T collectors are classified as either air-based or water-based, depending on the thermal fluid used to extract thermal energy from the panel. BIPV/T collectors use concentrated solar energy as compared to the conventional multi-crystalline-Si PV cells, which helps in utilizing more space, increasing watt per material needed, and reducing cost. "Thermal concentrators offer several benefits over conventional collectors, such as utilizing more space, providing a greater degree of power density and thus raising the temperature of the fluid, and reducing the area of the hottest components" (Abdelrazik, Shboul, Elwardany, Zohny, & Osama, 2022). Water-based BIPV/T is usually a single unit that is placed on a wall or roof of a building. The structure usually consists of a glass cover for the outside, water pipes, air space, a heat insulation layer, and a thermal absorber (Abdelrazik, Shboul, Elwardany, Zohny, & Osama, 2022). For instance, we can build suburban communities that include BIPV/T technologies with battery storage. These suburban communities can be connected to the grid in the case of necessity; however, BIPV/T will drastically reduce the need for electricity made from fossil fuels. However, this approach does not work for every single area as many controlled and uncontrolled factors are involved with the use of BIPV/T technology.

Agriculture applications

Due to the modern era, many people do not think about collecting food any further than their local grocery market. However, there is an entire industry of agriculture that builds and maintains our nation. Same with any other field, there are many technological advancements in this industry. From huge machinery to new automatic tools. Solar energy is used for irrigation for crops. A microprocessor-controlled solar energy system is used in an electrical motor to operate an irrigation system (Kannan & Vakeesan, 2016). The microprocessor is used to program discharge rate and irrigation intervals to distribute an optimal level of crop water, and to use solar energy most efficiently. The solar energy system can include a storage battery to use when solar energy is not up to par. Since the electrical motor is not connected to the electrical grid, it can stay active (Kannan & Vakeesan, 2016). However, the efficiency of the machine or the photovoltaic cell is influenced by many factors, including, temperature, solar irradiance, and dust (Sampaio & González, 2017). The pumping system consists of a microprocessor, which can be programmed to the soil moisture level, to effectively water the crops with the least amount of resource wastage. Similarly, solar energy is used for greenhouses. A greenhouse is a structure built for the intensive care of crops for better production. Fortunately, new solar technologies allow the greenhouse to use solar energy for both electricity and heat (Kannan & Vakeesan, 2016). It uses an array of PV panels on the roof to collect solar energy, which is then transferred to a solar array combiner box and onwards until the AC circuit breakers provide electricity to the utility interface (Kannan & Vakeesan, 2016). This system can assist in greatly reducing the need for fossil fuel for heating the greenhouses, where gas or oil heaters are used to release CO2 for better plant growth (Kannan & Vakeesan, 2016).

However, the system is very expensive and many industries struggle with adapting to solar energy due to its recent advancements and its struggle to compete with conventional systems. (Timilsina et al., 2012). According to the Bureau of Reclamation, water covers 71% of the earth's surface but 3% of Earth's water is fresh, of which 0.5% is available (Basin, 2022). The other 2.5% of freshwater is "locked in glaciers, polar ice caps, atmosphere, and soil; highly polluted; or lies too far under the earth's surface to be extracted at an affordable cost" (Basin, 2022). Therefore, a process of desalination of salt water is done where freshwater is limited. Reverse osmosis is used in the process of desalination; however, it is a very expensive treatment that requires a large amount of energy. PV technology can be used to supply electricity to desalination plants and further help manage the freshwater demand of the world's growing population (Kannan & Vakeesan, 2016). Similarly, PV technology can aid wastewater treatment plants to supply electricity to operations that treat biochemical waste to eliminate environmental pollution and the excess use of fossil fuels (Kannan & Vakeesan, 2016). Lastly, solar energy is being used as a wonderful asset to space craft technologies. Solar energy is abundant in space, it is used for the creation of electrostatic discharge. Photovoltaic power is also incorporated in earth-orbiting space crafts at "low earth geosynchronous orbits", due to the environmental concern for nuclear power sources in space crafts (Kannan & Vakeesan, 2016). Furthermore, NASA is intending to use solar arrays for deep space emissions and future projects.

Moving forward

Despite the diverse applications of solar energy, there are huge barriers to the development and deployment of solar energy and its technologies. The barriers can be divided into three major groups; technological, financial, and institutional. Firstly, the photovoltaic cells' conversion efficiencies are low due to the limitation placed on the components, such as a battery, inverters, and the low supply of raw materials, such as silicon (Timilsina et al., 2012). Furthermore, every solar energy requires a storage component, usually in the form of batteries, to sustain the system when solar energy is not optimal. However, the short battery life span and the disposal of batteries are difficult when a structured disposal/recycling process is not standardized. In regards to solar thermal systems, the heat-carrying capacity of the heat transfer fluid and thermal losses are extremely limited (Timilsina et al., 2012). However, the recent advancement in BIPV/T water and air systems allows the limitation to decrease. "The applicability of frequently used convective heat transfer expressions was investigated. Semi-transparent rather than opaque PV, multiple inlets, and recentlydesigned flow deflectors were tested as thermal improvement approaches. The results revealed a thermal efficiency of up to 33% (Abdelrazik, Shboul, Elwardany, Zohny, & Osama, 2022). Secondly, the economic barriers start with the expensive initial system cost, which includes both manufacturing and installation process. Financial institutions consider solar energy technologies to be a high risk since solar energy projects have "shorter history, lengthy periods, and small revenue stream" (Timilsina et al., 2012). Thus, there are higher financial charges for solar energy projects and research.

Furthermore, the initial cost and slow revenue raise barriers against conventional systems which are usually more accessible and cheaper to set up. The cost is also influenced by the location, where less sunny locations require larger systems to generate the same amount of electricity as compared to a smaller system in a sunny location (Sampaio & González, 2017). Therefore, solar energy may be a bigger deterrent to countries with less sunny climates. The institutional barriers involve the novelty that the technology brings. There are limited institutional capacities for workforce training due to poor or lack of financial incentives and policies (Timilsina et al., 2012). Furthermore, existing laws and regulations constrain the deployment of solar energy and provide deterrents to those who want to research or invest. Lastly, solar panels are highly influenced by many uncontrollable factors, such as sunshine intensity, cloudiness, wind speed, and solar radiance.

Conclusion

Solar energy is one of the best ways to combat the increasing energy demands and climate change. The applications of solar energy are very diverse and range from a calculator using solar energy to large buildings being fully powered by it. Despite the huge barriers, researchers make huge efforts in the technologies of photovoltaic cells and solar energy systems and find new applications for solar energy. In the last 6 years, the advancement of BIPV/T has been enormous and is proof of the potential of solar energy (Abdelrazik et al., 2022). With technological advancements and significant contributions from the world, a future world can be built, fueled entirely by renewable energy.

References

Abdelrazik, A. S., Shboul, B., Elwardany, M., Zohny, R. N., & Osama, A. (2022). The recent advancements in the building integrated photovoltaic/thermal (BIPV/T) systems: An updated review. Renewable and Sustainable Energy Reviews, 170, 112988. doi: 10.1016/j.rser.2022.112988

Basin, C.-G. (2022). Water Facts - Worldwide Water Supply | ARWEC| CCAO | Area Offices | California-Great Basin | Bureau of Reclamation. Retrieved from Usbr.gov website: https://www.usbr.gov/mp/arwec/water-facts-ww-water-sup. html#:~:text=0.5%25%20of%20the%20earth's%20water,for%20 each%20person%20on%20earth.

Berrang-Ford, L., Ford, J. D., & Paterson, J. (2011). Are we adapting to climate change? Global Environmental Change, 21(1), 25–33. doi: 10.1016/j.gloenvcha.2010.09.012

Castillo-González, J., Comino, F., Navas-Martos, F. J., & Ruiz de Adana, M. (2022). Life cycle assessment of an experimental solar HVAC system and a conventional HVAC system. Energy and Buildings, 256, 111697. doi: 10.1016/j.enbuild.2021.111697

Dutta, R., Chanda, K., & Maity, R. (2022). Future of solar energy potential in a changing climate across the world: A CMIP6 multi-model ensemble analysis. Renewable Energy, 188, 819–829. doi: 10.1016/j.renene.2022.02.023

Indoor Air Quality | US EPA. (2017, November 2). Retrieved from US EPA website: https://www.epa.gov/report-environment/ indoor-air-quality#note1

Kannan, N., & Vakeesan, D. (2016). Solar energy for the future world: A review. Renewable and Sustainable Energy Reviews, 62, 1092–1105. doi: 10.1016/j.rser.2016.05.022

Masson, V., Bonhomme, M., Salagnac, J.-L., Briottet, X., & Lemonsu, A. (2014). Solar panels reduce both global warming and urban heat island. Frontiers in Environmental Science, 2. doi: 10.3389/fenvs.2014.00014

Rahman, S. M. A., Issa, S., El Haj Assad, M., Khaleduzzaman Shah, S., Abdelkareem, M. A., Enamul Hoque, Md., & Olabi, A. G. (2022). Performance enhancement and life cycle analysis of a novel solar HVAC system using underground water and energy recovery technique. Thermal Science and Engineering Progress, 36, 101515. doi: 10.1016/j.tsep.2022.101515

Sampaio, P. G. V., & González, M. O. A. (2017). Photovoltaic solar energy: Conceptual framework. Renewable and Sustainable Energy Reviews, 74, 590–601. doi: 10.1016/j.rser.2017.02.081

Timilsina, G. R., Kurdgelashvili, L., & Narbel, P. A. (2012). Solar energy: Markets, economics, and policies. Renewable and Sustainable Energy Reviews, 16(1), 449–465. doi: 10.1016/j. rser.2011.08.009

Chapter 7
Decentralized Energy

Hannah Nie

Climate change mitigation and adaptation require major changes to the energy sector to pivot away from fossil fuel consumption and transition into using more sustainable alternatives. This has led to the rise of alternative technologies and strategies, such as the concept of decentralized energy.

Decentralized energy is also known as distributed energy, and it describes alternative ways of using and distributing energy (Alstone, Gershenson, & Kammen, 2015). Traditionally, energy distribution has been dominated by large-scale, centralized systems which are often dependent on the generation of electricity through the consumption of fossil fuels (Alstone et al., 2015). For example, at a central power plant, electricity may be generated using diesel or natural gas, or by harnessing bodies of water for hydroelectricity. Following this, the electricity must then be transmitted to consumers through the grid (Venema & Cisse, 2004).

However, centralized energy distribution systems have several disadvantages. From the perspective of climate change prevention and adaptation, centralized energy is often intertwined with the use of non-renewable energy sources and does not allow for much flexibility in seeking out local, alternative sources of renewable energy (Alstone et al., 2015). Centralized energy takes a "one-size-fits-all" approach to electricity production and distribution, which can act as a barrier to the adoption of more flexible sustainable solutions, and ignores the local perspectives and challenges of different communities and geographical regions.

This leads to another significant shortcoming of centralized energy systems: despite their rapid growth and expansion over the years, centralized energy systems still have not been able to deliver electricity to all consumers in need. In fact, as of 2020, about 10% of the world's population still does not have access to electricity (The World Bank, n.d.-a). Rural communities and poorer regions are often part of these underserved groups which lack access to electricity (Alstone et al., 2015), showing the presence of certain inequities and barriers to accessing this key resource. A variety of different factors may contribute to this gap in access to electricity. One that is perhaps the most obvious is the challenge of physically connecting rural communities to the central grid, especially those situated in remote locations (Alstone et al., 2015), or geographical barriers such as mountain ranges, or bodies of water, in the case of island nations (Kempener et al., 2015). Centralized energy systems are limited by their need for physical infrastructure to deliver electricity, sometimes over very long distances, which can be costly (Alstone et al., 2015). Social and political factors may also play a role, as this infrastructure may require funding or approval from governmental organizations, therefore, marginalized groups may lack the power or influence to advocate for themselves to gain access to electricity (Alstone et al., 2015).

Ultimately, inequities in access to electricity directly lead to other adverse effects in these vulnerable groups. Notably, rural communities which lack access to electricity often resort to using less efficient and at times dangerous sources of energy, such as burning biomass, including wood, crop residues, and manure, to meet their basic needs (Venema & Cisse, 2004). The burning of biomass, such as in primitive wood stoves, is one of the most severe sources of chronic air pollution which releases toxic substances including smoke, carbon monoxide, methane, and numerous carcinogens that will in turn inflict further damage upon the environment and human health (Venema & Cisse, 2004). These inefficient methods of energy generation also involve significant resource demands in terms of human labor and natural materials, often non-renewable, which puts further strain on these communities and their natural environments, reinforcing a cycle of poverty and preventing the development of a greater capacity for climate change adaptation and resilience among these vulnerable groups (Venema & Cisse, 2004).

Decentralized energy offers a potential solution to replace or supplement our current system of energy distribution. The paradigm of decentralized energy envisions a system in which power generation takes place on a small scale and at a local level, relatively close to consumers (Venema & Cisse, 2004). Instead of using large-scale, nationwide electrical grids, decentralized energy involves the use of mini-grids, which are small-scale electrical networks that deliver 10 kW - 10 MW of power, or even micro-grids, which deliver 1 - 10 kW of power, that is generated and distributed locally, independent from the central grid (Johnson & Muhoza, 2016). Decentralized energy systems can also operate completely separately from any electrical grid through the use of home power generation systems (Kempener et al., 2015).

The proximity of energy sources to consumers improves efficiency by reducing energy loss associated with long-distance energy transmission, and could also help make electricity more accessible to more people by providing more realistic modes of delivery to remote regions (Kempener et al., 2015). Decentralized energy also takes a more flexible approach than centralized energy by considering local resources and features that can be leveraged using new technologies to generate energy efficiently to meet local demands.

Decentralized energy is often associated with the use of renewable energy sources. Renewable energy sources are diverse and often vary depending on the features of the local region, for example, factors such as sun exposure or wind speed can dictate the suitability of a region for solar or wind power generation. Moreover, despite technological advancements, there are still limitations to the reliability of renewable energy sources, and power generation from these sources may be intermittent or low voltage. Decentralized energy presents a unique opportunity to make renewable energy a feasible reality for communities in need as it allows for the integration of various diverse local power generation systems, which can supplement one another to provide a steady source of electricity together (Sabri, El Kamoun, & Lakrami, 2019).

The International Renewable Energy Agency (IRENA) reports that as of 2013, hydropower was the most commonly used power source in decentralized mini-grids, accounting for 75 GW of power generated in such systems globally, while diesel was the second largest source, generating 23 GW of power (Kempener et al., 2015). Note that while decentralized energy systems present a prime opportunity for renewable energy, nonrenewable sources have also been used in such systems, often acting as a backup power source for networks with unreliable power supplies (Kempener et al., 2015).

Initially, the implementation of solar and wind energy in decentralized systems lagged in comparison to hydropower and diesel, but their prevalence has increased over time. In particular, technological advancements in the solar energy sector have made it increasingly accessible and effective. Photovoltaic equipment has evolved to have higher performance and lower costs while being relatively scalable and accessible compared to the infrastructural demands of centralized energy sources (Alstone et al., 2015). Solar power is also very versatile and amenable to adaptation for various small-scale applications, such as solar-powered lights or solar home systems, in addition to typical solar-powered mini-grids (Off-Grid Renewable Energy Statistics 2022, n.d., p. 202). According to the IRENA, the amount of off-grid power generated through solar energy sources has increased significantly over time, with widespread usage, for instance in the case of solar-powered lights, which were used by approximately 112, 056,000 people worldwide, compared to 7,196,000 people worldwide who were connected to off-grid hydropower (Off-Grid Renewable Energy Statistics 2022, n.d.).

Other renewable energy sources that may be used in decentralized energy systems include biomass, geothermal, and hybrids of different energy sources, such as solar wind or solar-diesel hybrid systems (Kempener et al., 2015). Notably, hybrid systems can help ease the transition to renewable energy by supplementing non-renewable energy with renewable energy, for example in hybrids of diesel power and renewable sources (Kempener et al., 2015).

Decentralized energy around the world

Decentralized energy is particularly suitable for meeting the energy needs of rural or remote regions, and providing low-cost solutions for communities that still do not have access to electricity. The majority of people currently lacking electricity access reside in developing countries of Asia and Africa (Cozzi, Wetzel, Tonolo, & Hyppolite, 2022), and efforts to implement decentralized energy systems in these areas are underway.

Microgrid and mini-grid installation have experienced rapid growth in Asia over the past years (Kempener et al., 2015). According to the World Bank, over 16,000 mini-grids had been installed in Asia as of 2019, accounting for 85% of the world's mini-grids (The World Bank, n.d.-b). In terms of renewable decentralized energy, there is a particularly large solar lantern market in Asia, with up to 3.2 million units sold in 2011, mostly accounted for by India (Kempener et al., 2015). In 2015, Bangladesh saw a unique boom in solar home systems driven by governmental support, accounting for 3 million of the 6 million solar home systems installed globally (Kempener et al., 2015).

China has been a leader in the adoption of renewable decentralized energy, having been involved in renewable energy-based mini-grids since the 1950s, which have mostly consisted of hydropower systems (Kempener et al., 2015). As of 2012, China was also a leading country in small wind turbine-powered mini-grids, harboring 39% of turbines installed globally (Kempener et al., 2015).

Moreover, decentralized photovoltaic and solar photovoltaic-diesel hybrid power systems have played a unique role in providing electricity to schools in Malaysia, specifically on the island of Borneo, where connection to the centralized grid had been difficult (UNESCAP, n.d.). The Malaysian government financed the installation of photovoltaic and photovoltaic diesel hybrid systems at 63 schools in the region, which supported lighting, computer use, and Internet access for students (UNESCAP, n.d.).

Decentralized solar energy has also been proposed to have great potential specifically in southeast Asia, among countries like Cambodia, Laos, and Thailand (Siala, Chowdhury, Dang, & Galelli, 2021). Due to their proximity to the Mekong River, these countries have historically relied on centralized systems based on hydropower (Siala et al., 2021). However, hydro dams are damaging to the local ecosystems and biodiversity (Siala et al., 2021). Recent analyses show that the use of renewable energy sources in local areas, especially solar power, can offer a cost-effective alternative power source to help meet energy demands and ultimately reduce the need for dam construction (Siala et al., 2021).

In Africa, Morocco has been a leading country in mini-grid installation, having installed renewable energy-based mini-grids in over 3,600 villages, serving nearly 52,000 households as of 2010 (Kempener et al., 2015). Moreover, Nigeria, Tanzania, Kenya, and Rwanda have been identified as countries with high potential for decentralized energy systems (Kempener et al., 2015). Senegal, Nigeria, and Tanzania are among the top 5 countries in terms of the number of planned mini-grid installations as of 2019 (The World Bank, n.d.-b).

Senegal has also had prior success in solar-powered decentralized energy systems, dating back to 1987 in a five-year partnership with Germany (Venema & Cisse, 2004). Through this project, the German government helped fund the implementation of local photovoltaic systems in the rural communities of two villages in Senegal: Ndiébel and Diaoulé (Venema & Cisse, 2004). The rural villages of Senegal, like many other regions of Africa, are often disconnected from central energy systems and lack the infrastructure to become connected, which leads them to depend on burning biomass for energy (Venema & Cisse, 2004). This contributes to growing rates of deforestation and ecological damage, which can be exacerbated by other forms of human activity, such as land clearing for agriculture, as well as threats related to climate change, such as increasing droughts (Venema & Cisse, 2004).

Two village-wide solar power stations were established, as well as over 1,300 smaller Solar Home Stations (Venema & Cisse, 2004). Some of the solar power stations were also equipped with water pumping capabilities, offering another functionality that provided unique advantages to help support local needs for water, improving sanitation and agriculture (Venema & Cisse, 2004). With these new resources, electricity became the main power source for lighting in the village and was also greatly used for radios, television, cassette recorders, and refrigerators (Venema & Cisse, 2004). In the community, increased reliability of lighting via decentralized energy sources also helped improve healthcare facilities, supporting surgical operations, infant deliveries, and other procedures (Venema & Cisse, 2004). Following the success of this program, a similar initiative was carried out later on in partnership with the government of Japan (Venema & Cisse, 2004).

Islands such as the world's 38 small island developing nations (SIDS) make up another group that could specifically benefit from the use of renewable decentralized energy (The World Bank, 2022). Fossil fuels must be imported to islands, often at very high costs, which can amount to as much as 20% of the national GDPs of small island nations (The World Bank, 2022). Archipelagos or countries which have populations residing on multiple different small islands face further complications in electricity delivery due to these geographical barriers which prevent the establishment of a fully connected and centralized national electrical grid (The World Bank, 2022). Therefore, decentralized systems can help supply energy to these disparate island communities independently, through local renewable sources which can help to cut back on the usage of financially and environmentally costly fossil fuels.

In 2012, the IRENA estimated that the world's SIDS had installed decentralized electrical grids with a capacity of 28.4 GW in total, with Singapore, Cuba, and the Dominican Republic taking the lead in decentralized energy capacity (Kempener et al., 2015). Later in 2018, Palau, a small island nation found in the Pacific Ocean, announced that it would be launching the world's largest microgrid, in an initiative called the Armonia project, in partnership with a French company called Engie SA (News, n.d.). The Armonia project microgrid has a capacity of 35 MW from solar power, and 45 MWh of energy storage capacity (News, n.d.). Decentralized energy seems to be an apt solution to help address unique challenges such as those posed by Palau's geographical situation. Palau is made up of 340 islands, and while approximately 70% of Palau's population lives on Koror, its main island, many communities are spread out throughout the rest of the nation's islands (National Geographic, 2014; News, n.d.). Renewable energy-based microgrids can help deliver electricity to Palau's remote communities and reduce their reliance on imported fossil fuels, which also helps Palau work towards its pledged goal of increasing the proportion of renewable sources in the nation's energy usage, from 6% at the time of the establishment of the Paris Agreement, to 45% by 2025 (News, n.d.).

With this overview of decentralized energy and its applications, it is clear that this emerging system can help to fulfill the unmet needs of various diverse populations around the world, and its reach continues to increase with upcoming projects and technological progress in the field.

Smart grids and other decentralized energy technologies

Additionally, some other considerations relating to the use of decentralized energy systems in the future moving forward include the technology necessary to control energy flow in such systems (Alstone et al., 2015). Centralized energy systems use centralized controllers to coordinate the distribution of electricity to different regions, however, these traditional strategies will need to be adapted to the heterogenous, and complex nature of decentralized energy systems (Sabri et al., 2019). Decentralized systems often operate using microgrids which must connect numerous small-scale power generators and local electrical loads and energy storage units. It is often difficult for one central controller to facilitate communication and coordinate energy distribution between the various elements of a microgrid.

An alternative approach that has been used is that of decentralized control, where each local power generation system has its controller that acts independently of all other controllers (Sabri et al., 2019). This approach has its shortcomings because, without communication between local controllers, each controller will only operate based on information from their part of the grid, and would tend to transfer the extra load to neighbouring grids, leading to an overload of the entire system due to the lack of coordination, which was seen in August of 2003, when a mass blackout took place across North America (Sabri et al., 2019).

Current efforts have been directed towards the development of smart grids, which use computer algorithms to help control energy flow in an efficient way dependent on local energy usage and needs (Alstone et al., 2015). Advancements in communication technologies make it possible to design improved systems that combine elements of centralized and decentralized control, which can be described as "distributed control" (Sabri et al., 2019). In this approach, local controllers can communicate with a few neighbouring controllers, resulting in a communication network that allows for more feasible and effective overall control in the decentralized energy system (Sabri et al., 2019).

Mini-grids are often installed supplementary to a centralized grid (Sabri et al., 2019). In normal circumstances, the mini-grid will be connected to the centralized grid, but some mini-grids can also disconnect from the central system, entering an "islanded" state in which the mini-grid can operate completely independently of the central system (Sabri et al., 2019). While the islanded mode is not essential to all mini-grids or microgrids, it is a desired feature as it can improve the stability and reliability of such systems (Hatziargyriou, 2014). However, the switch from the grid-connected to the islanded mode requires major changes in the control system, and the islanded mode typically involves much more complex considerations which will require improved computation strategies to manage effectively (Sabri et al., 2019).

Smart grid technologies have allowed for improved applications of decentralized energy systems. An example of this can be seen in Hartley Bay, a remote community in British Columbia, Canada, which harbours Canada's first smart remote microgrid (Government of Canada, 2014). Hartley Bay had already installed local microgrids and sought to improve its system by using smart meters and smart controllers to help monitor and regulate their energy management more effectively and aid in the shift away from diesel towards renewable energy (Government of Canada, 2014). For instance, in 2010 they installed demand response systems in several commercial buildings that had high energy consumption within the community, which helped control energy demands during peak periods via manual and automatic adjustments (Government of Canada, 2014). Overall, the changes that they had adopted were estimated to have saved 77,000 liters of diesel per year, and further usage of demand response systems had the potential to save an additional 27,000 liters of diesel per year (Government of Canada, 2014). Overall, new strategies and technologies in this area could help further improve the effectiveness and reliability of energy distribution in decentralized energy systems.

In conclusion, the future of decentralized energy is promising and offers many alternative avenues to help us adapt and prevent the consequences of climate change by easing the transition to renewable energy sources and promoting more efficient energy usage. Decentralized energy is a growing field that can greatly improve electricity access to populations who are most in need, which will also ultimately help support their resilience and ability to adapt to climate change.

References

Alstone, P., Gershenson, D., & Kammen, D. M. (2015). Decentralized energy systems for clean electricity access. Nature Climate Change, 5(4), 305–314. doi: 10.1038/nclimate2512

Cozzi, L., Wetzel, D., Tonolo, G., & Hyppolite, J. (2022, November 3). For the first time in decades, the number of people without access to electricity is set to increase in 2022. Retrieved from International Energy Agency website: https://www.iea.org/commentaries/for-the-first-time-in-decades-the-number-of-people-without-access-to-electricity-is-set-to-increase-in-2022

Government of Canada. (2014, January 15). The First Canadian Smart Remote Microgrid: Hartley Bay, BC. Retrieved from Natural Resources Canada website: https://www.nrcan.gc.ca/maps-tools-publications/publications/energy-publications/technology-research-publications/first-canadian-smart-remote-microgrid-hartley-bay-bc/14421

Hatziargyriou, N. (2014). Microgrids: Architectures and Control. John Wiley & Sons. Retrieved from https://books.google.ca/books?hl=fr&lr=&id=ywxzAgAAQBAJ&oi=fnd&pg=PR13&ots=9rvbByLvu5&sig=QZDdngp4FNE5sEKr_PGlL0NPSUg&rediresc=y#v=onepage& q&f=false

Johnson, O., & Muhoza, C. (2016). Renewable energy mini-grids: An alternative approach to energy access in southern Africa. Stockholm Environment Institute. Retrieved from Stockholm Environment Institute website: https://www.jstor.org/stable/resrep02777

Kempener, R., d'Ortigue, O. L., Saygin, D., Skeer, J., Vinci, S., & Gielen, D. (2015). Off-grid renewable energy systems: Status and methodological issues [Working Paper]. International Renewable Energy Agency.

Off-grid renewable energy statistics 2022. (n.d.).

Sabri, Y., El Kamoun, N., & Lakrami, F. (2019). A Survey: Centralized, Decentralized, and Distributed Control Scheme in Smart Grid Systems. 2019 7th Mediterranean Congress of Telecommunications (CMT), 1–11. doi: 10.1109/CMT.2019.8931370

Siala, K., Chowdhury, A. K., Dang, T. D., & Galelli, S. (2021). Solar energy and regional coordination as a feasible alternative to large hydropower in Southeast Asia. Nature Communications, 12(1), 4159. doi: 10.1038/s41467-021-24437-6

The World Bank. (n.d.). Access to electricity (% of the population). Retrieved from The World Bank website: https://data.worldbank.org/indicator/EG.ELC.ACCS.ZS?end=2020&start=1990&view=chart

The World Bank. (n.d.). Mini Grids for Half a Billion People: Market Outlook and Handbook for Decision Makers [Text/HTML]. Retrieved from World Bank website: https://www.worldbank.org/en/topic/energy/publication/mini-grids-for-half-a-billion-people

UNESCAP. (n.d.). Fact Sheet—Decentralized Energy System. Retrieved from https://www.unescap.org/sites/default/files/14.%20FS-Decentralized-energy-system.pdf

Venema, H. D., & Cisse, M. (Eds.). (2004). Seeing the light: Adapting to climate change with decentralized renewable energy in developing countries. Winnipeg: International Institute for Sustainable Development: Climate Change Knowledge Network.

Chapter 8

Transportation

Rawan Ahmed

Introduction

Climate change is a major global challenge that is already affecting the planet in several ways, including rising temperatures, more frequent and severe natural disasters, and sea level rise. As a result, transportation systems must adapt to minimise their greenhouse gas emissions and become more resilient to the impacts of climate change.

Transportation Companies

Warmer temperatures, more frequently occurring and severe extreme weather events, and lower availability of natural resources, as a result of climate change, will raise pressure on transportation businesses to adjust to new rules and consumer concerns, as well as dangers to assets and infrastructure. The sources of this pressure vary, ranging from those facing direct climate change dangers to those advocating for proactive asset management and important components of global supply networks. The transportation industry plays a vital role in facilitating and driving global climate change adaptation measures within these supply networks. The transportation sector is especially sensitive to the physical consequences of climate change across its supply chain, both in terms of assets (such as ocean freighters and railcars) and places (such as airports and seaports). Rising sea levels, temperature fluctuations, and extreme weather occurrences are among its primary vulnerabilities, all of which can have an impact on destinations and activities (Finley & Ryan Schuchard, 2011). Through transportation adaptation strategies, the sector has the potential to play a more comprehensive strategic role in addressing the majority of sectors' supply chain impacts. However, because this capability is frequently dependent on existing transportation infrastructure, strategic infrastructure expenditures are a top priority. The transportation sector should be concerned about proactive and responsible adaptation for the following reasons. Rising sea levels, extreme weather events, and changes in weather patterns all pose serious and immediate challenges to transportation companies' supply networks, causing commercial disruptions. (Finley & Ryan Schuchard, 2011) As a result, businesses with supply chains in coastal areas, flood zones, or high-risk storm sites may incur higher rates of disruption and delay. Climate change's physical concerns may impair transportation operations, including facilities and assets. Rising sea levels, for example, will overwhelm seaports that have not taken necessary adaptation measures, forcing them to close temporarily or permanently. External demand from authorities, consumers, and shareholders for prompt analysis and action on climate concerns is causing rapid transformation in the sector. Simultaneously, the industry is linked to extremely sensitive infrastructure systems, frequently controlled by the government, which will necessitate long-term planning and cooperation for effective climate-ready systems (Finley & Ryan Schuchard, 2011).

Companies are using insurance plans to cover the physical risks that climate change poses to their supply chains, locations, and capacity to deliver services on time. Cintra has included global climate change patterns in the design of its insurance plans, coverage, and premium rates. Electrocomponents has obtained business interruption insurance to help protect its supply chain and operational risks from delays caused by climate change impacts. Physical threats are monitored regularly en route and at important site sites. Climate-related hazards are often assessed as part of standard risk assessments, with follow-up measures incorporated into business continuity planning (Finley & Ryan Schuchard, 2011). Cobham conducted site risk assessments, including in-depth analyses of high-risk locations, to identify and implement appropriate climate adaptation measures to equipment and infrastructure. To identify and better understand future hazards, National Express Group conducted particular climate change risk assessments using the U.K. Climate Impacts Programme models. Companies are increasingly engaging in comprehensive plans to link their existing CSR initiatives with their specific climate adaption goals, resulting in more significant internal efficiency and alignment, as well as increased preparation for a low-carbon society (Finley & Ryan Schuchard, 2011). Auckland International Airport has established an integrated sustainability strategy and action plan that addresses climate change challenges across the value chain, positioning sustainable business practices as the way ahead. This strategy was created to supplement New Zealand's future climate change adaptation needs. To accelerate the company's efforts toward climate change adaptation, Boeing created detailed strategic measures and procedures. The organization has developed and is actively working toward reduction objectives and efficiency goals through a defined internal governance framework, which will result in cost savings, a decreased carbon footprint, and possibly positive brand effects. The corporation has concentrated heavily on biofuels and boosting aviation efficiency.

Companies are developing the next generation of transportation and logistics technologies to support sustainable behaviour and reduce greenhouse gas (GHG) emissions through smart investments (Finley & Ryan Schuchard, 2011). Deutsche Post DHL has created a portfolio of green logistics solutions and carbon-neutral products for their clients to not only communicate knowledge about climate change but also to equip them with decision-making resources. One business-led effort incorporates CO_2 into supply chain architecture, allowing executives to select the carbon-reduction scenario that best meets their operational, cost, and carbon needs. The green product range is part of Deutsche Post DHL's GoGreen environmental protection initiative, which aims to reduce the company's environmental effects and improve its carbon efficiency. MTU Aero Engines is concentrating on decreasing fuel consumption, as well as CO_2 and NOx emissions, through initiatives in research and development such as their geared turbofan technology and intercooler recuperative aero-engine, which may advantageously position the firm as a vendor for the airline industry's transition to a more sustainable model. The transportation industry, as a logistics and planning firm, has discovered the unique potential in developing and deploying improved logistics and efficiency technologies both internally and externally (Finley & Ryan Schuchard, 2011). Ryder System Inc. and other firms have seen the potential to improve disaster relief logistics. Climate change is projected to increase the need for such measures. United Parcel Service Inc. has created many innovative logistics techniques to cut GHG emissions and shift industry leadership toward future adaptability. UPS's key successes include the Package Flow Technologies initiative, which avoided more than 100 million miles of travel, as well as the company's fuel reduction systems and aircraft technology. UPS has also changed toward a high rate of intermodal downshift, in which the corporation may carry the same items using several modes of transportation to cut emissions.

Recommendations for Transportation Companies

Transportation firms are well-positioned to help their sector enhance logistics and transportation innovation and have a significant multiplier effect across the supply chain. Companies with leading logistical practices and external sustainability solutions will have a significant competitive advantage as energy reporting, including the CDP, rises. As a new service offering, companies may explore developing proprietary or public tools and sustainable logistical solutions for clients (Finley & Ryan Schuchard, 2011). Finally, as many organizations have realized as a result of catastrophic occurrences such as Hurricane Katrina, heat waves in Europe, and increased tsunami activity throughout the world, disaster response is a critical chance to harness industry experience. Transportation networks in badly damaged areas may entirely shut down, necessitating other networks to aid in immediate disaster response activities as well as cleanup and rehabilitation work (Finley & Ryan Schuchard, 2011). As the demand for disaster aid grows across the world, the transportation industry may play an important role in enhancing responsiveness.

Transportation industries are already seeing insurance coverage retractions due to extremely sensitive assets. Companies will be better protected from future financial risks if they are proactive in analyzing climate hazards to operations and fully incorporating them into insurance plans. The complexity of the transportation business and the diversity of many transportation enterprises give an excellent potential for innovation. Companies that leverage internal knowledge, as well as strategic alliances for technology development, are already experiencing higher returns and increased client variety (Finley & Ryan Schuchard, 2011). New technology can give answers to the sector by incorporating not just reduction methods but also an understanding of climate change issues into product creation. Technologies such as America

Latina Logistica's rail line detector for fractures caused by temperature variations offers prospects for both asset protection and the development of new services and products for the sector as a whole.

Seaport CDP reports were disproportionately low, reflecting broader sector tendencies of low levels of risk identification and much lower rates of proactive management. Because seaports are crucial points in major supply networks, inadequate planning for increasing sea levels poses a direct danger to the shipping and rail industries, as well as tourism and retail. The absence of direct jurisdiction over seaports, as well as the wide range of projections for sea-level rise, have been portrayed as impediments to industry development toward climate-resilient seaports (Finley & Ryan Schuchard, 2011). As a result, strategic planning for climate change mitigation has an immediate need and role within climate adaptation for the transportation industry. As the media and reporting bodies such as the CDP focus more on climate change mitigation measures, adaptation programs will become more relevant. Companies may demonstrate their proactive efforts by actively discussing adaption initiatives through external reporting methods like the CDP, as well as CSR reports and online communications (Finley & Ryan Schuchard, 2011). This also emphasizes the significance of adaptability and the acceptance of responsibility within the organization to address the issue. Due to the extended lifespan of transportation infrastructure, corporations and government agencies alike are finding it vital to exhibit climate change adaptation thinking in their long-term planning and investments. Transportation businesses must consider these ideas through the perspective of their responsibilities in the transportation network. The climate adaption plan of an airport will differ from that of a training firm. Regardless, transportation businesses are well-positioned to adapt and develop climate policies and solutions that will spread throughout a wide range of supply chains.

Promote Sustainable Mobility

Managing the mobility of people and goods is one of the most difficult environmental and social challenges of our time. However, sustainable mobility offers compelling answers to climate change. By 2030, passenger traffic will exceed 80,000 billion passenger-kilometer and freight volume will grow by 70 percent globally (Mahmoud Mohieldin & Nancy Vandycke, 2017). Billions of people in fast-growing regions such as India, China, Sub-Saharan Africa, and Southeast Asia will have higher lifestyle expectations and new mobility aspirations. Through maritime links and physical roads, megaprojects like China's One Belt, One Road will connect more than half of the world's population and roughly a quarter of the goods and services that move around the world. A long-term perspective focused on sustainability is a defining factor in the future of mobility. Nonetheless, transportation was not endorsed as a distinct global Sustainable Development Goal (SDG), owing to the sector's inability to speak with a unified voice to influence this global process. Some aspects of transportation have been included in various SDGs (for example, road safety, carbon emissions, and so on), and the international community has made several commitments related to transportation over the last two years. For example, transportation is a key policy component of the action plan agreed upon by landlocked developing countries to transition them to land-linked states (Mahmoud Mohieldin & Nancy Vandycke, 2017). The transportation sector has the potential to improve the lives and livelihoods of billions of people—their health, environment, and quality of life—as well as to stabilize climate change.

However, it is currently heading in the wrong direction, with transportation contributing to gross inequalities in access to economic and social opportunities, rising numbers of deaths from transport-related accidents, intensive fossil fuel use, massive emissions of greenhouse gasses, and air and noise pollution. The social, environmental, and economic challenges are apparent. However, there is still a leadership vacuum at the global level, with no clear set of principles for transforming the sector. There is a way forward, but it will require collaboration from all stakeholders. For starters, the industry can no longer accept a fragmented approach. It is time to strengthen coherence and speak with one voice to impact global and national operations. The current approach, in which a plethora of stakeholder agencies, multilateral development banks, the manufacturing industry, civil society, etc. act independently, has failed to bring the scale of actions and financing to transform mobility. It is not impossible to bring these disparate actors together. In 2010, the energy sector partners embarked on the same journey, allowing energy to be mainstreamed into all global agreements on sustainable development while also gaining the credibility and reliability needed to attract private and development finance partners (Mahmoud Mohieldin & Nancy Vandycke, 2017).

Furthermore, the economic assessment of transportation projects should be drastically altered. Traditional cost-benefit analyses of such projects focus on reduced travel time as a proxy for efficiency. However, there is a trade-off between, say, speed and fatalities. Crash costs can offset the expected efficiency gains from increasing transportation speeds. Integrating other sustainability dimensions, such as safety, green characteristics, and inclusivity, will have a significant impact on project evaluation and, as a result, transform project design – and this is the right way forward. No road project, for example, should be funded without taking safety, equity, and climate impact into account. Prioritizing sustainability in an economic evaluation of transport projects can transform project design (Savant, 2022).

Steps for Individuals to Take

Individuals' carbon footprint is adversely impacting the environment. Many people are seeking ways to reduce their carbon footprint. Individually, transportation is one of the worst offenders. Rising temperatures, year-round rain showers, tropical storms, wildfires, melting ice caps, and other unusual climate changes are the result of increased CO_2 emissions. Plant growth patterns are influenced by changing precipitation patterns. As a result, indigenous vegetation is migrating to cooler climates. As sea levels rise, shorelines erode and ecosystems are destroyed. All of this results in the displacement of various coastal cities and towns, as well as the total disappearance of certain islands and island nations. The Deep Decarbonization Pathways Project determined that to hold the global temperature rise to 2°C or less, everyone on earth will need to average an annual carbon footprint of 1.87 tons by 2050 (Cho, 2020). However, there are various ways for individuals to reduce fuel emissions and create a positive impact on the environment.

Use more environmentally friendly transportation: Biking, walking, carpooling, and taking public transportation can all help to reduce greenhouse gas emissions dramatically. In addition, people can make an effort to check with employers to see if they provide commuter benefits for public transportation or carpooling. Businesses can also use the Smart Location Calculator to take into account workplace locations and reduce commuting time for their employees.

Drive responsibly: Improve your fuel economy by driving slowly and carefully, using cruise control, and keeping your car in good condition. Avoid unnecessary braking and acceleration if you must drive. According to some studies, aggressive driving consumes 40% more fuel than consistent, calm driving (Cho, 2020).

Consider models with higher miles per gallon to find an energy-efficient vehicle: Individuals can reach for The EPA's Green Vehicle Guide which contains information on the cleanest, most fuel-efficient vehicles.

Switch to an electric vehicle: Plug-in electric vehicles typically emit fewer greenhouse gasses than a new gasoline-powered car. To see the emissions savings from driving an electric vehicle in your area, individuals can use the Beyond Tailpipe Emissions Calculator. Electric vehicles are a more environmentally friendly option than gasoline-powered vehicles. They reduce air pollution and the use of fossil fuels because there are no tailpipe emissions. Electric vehicles, followed by hybrid vehicles, emit less carbon dioxide than gasoline-powered vehicles. However, it is critical to consider the source of power used to charge the car because there are associated emissions that extend beyond the tailpipe. Electricity generated by coal power, for example, emits more greenhouse gasses than nuclear, hydropower, nuclear energy, solar power, and wind energy. Use low-emissions electricity sources for charging whenever possible.

Select an energy-efficient electric vehicle charger: People can take the time to learn about Energy Star electric vehicle chargers and incentives for electric and plug-in vehicles.

Make fewer trips: When running errands, plan to reduce driving time. Which journeys can be combined? Individuals can engage in activities such as grouping errands to make fewer trips and teleworking, if available, can reduce both fuel use and greenhouse gas emissions.

Take public transit: In addition to lowering your carbon footprint and saving an estimated 4.2 billion gallons of gasoline per year in the United States, taking public transportation reduces car ownership, often saves money, and helps prevent air pollution (Lozanova, 2018).

Bring something to read along for the ride, or simply relax and let someone else drive. In many areas, apps now make it easier than ever to know when trains or buses will arrive, saving time.

Air travel: For individuals who consistently fly for business or pleasure, air travel is most likely the source of the majority of their carbon footprint. If possible, avoid flying; on shorter trips, driving may emit fewer greenhouse gasses. Consider flying nonstop because landings and takeoffs consume more fuel and emit more emissions. Take the economy class. Because the carbon emissions of a flight are shared among more passengers in the economy, business class is responsible for nearly three times as many emissions as economy; first-class seats can result in nine times more carbon emissions than economy-class seats (Cho, 2020).

Get politically active: The most effective climate change solutions require government action, so vote. Become politically active and advocate representatives to take action as soon as possible to phase out the use of fossil fuels and decarbonize the country.

Offset carbon emissions: A carbon offset is a sum of money that can be used to fund a project that reduces greenhouse gas emissions somewhere else. If an individual offsets one tonne of carbon, they are assisting in the capture or destruction of one tonne of greenhouse gasses that would otherwise be released into the atmosphere. Offsets also encourage sustainable development and the utilization of renewable energy.

Conclusion

Transportation is an important part of the Canadian economy and society because it connects people and goods. Motorized transportation, on the other hand, has negative health and environmental consequences. Initiatives to reduce vehicle, engine, and fuel emissions can have a significant positive impact on air quality, acid rain, smog, and climate change. Governments must be committed to protecting the environment and people's health by implementing measures to reduce vehicle emissions. This includes developing vehicle and engine regulations, promoting sustainable transportation options, ensuring efficient modes of transportation, and encouraging better land-use planning and practices. Everyone must adopt eco-friendly habits and practices to fight against climate change.

References

Cho, R. (2020, December 30). The 35 Easiest Ways to Reduce Your Carbon Footprint. State of the Planet. Retrieved from https://news.climate.columbia.edu/2018/12/27/35-ways-reduce-carbon-footprint/

Finley, & Ryan Schuchard. (2011). Adapting to Climate Change: A Guide for the Transportation Industry. Business for Social Responsibility. Retrieved from https://www.bsr.org/reports/BSR_Climate_Adaptation_Issue_Brief_Transportation.pdf

Lozanova, S. (2018, April 18). Reduce Your Carbon Footprint: Transportation. Earth911. Retrieved from https://earth911.com/eco-tech/carbon-footprint-transportation/

Mohieldin, M., & Vandycke, N. (2017, July 11). Sustainable Mobility for the 21st Century. Retrieved from https://www.worldbank.org/en/news/feature/2017/07/10/sustainable-mobility-for-the-21st-century

Savant, S. (2022, December 19). Sustainable mobility: Why it offers compelling answers to climate change. Firstpost. Retrieved from https://www.firstpost.com/opinion/sustainable-mobility-why-it-offers-compelling-answers-to-climate-change-11836251.html

Chapter 9
Extreme Weather Protection

Zarmminaa Rehman

The phenomenon of climate change is real and the effects of it are becoming more frequent and more extreme. Protection against these extreme weather events is needed for ecology, infrastructure, and health and innovative solutions through the use of technology have pioneered a new era of combatting this change in our global climate.

Introduction

Climate change is the long-term alteration of the Earth's climate, particularly its temperature. Over the last century, the Earth's average temperature has risen significantly, leading to more frequent and severe extreme weather events (United Nations, 2022). These events include, but are not limited to, flooding related to extreme precipitation, hurricanes, and coastal storms, droughts, wildfires, winter storms, thunderstorms (Bell et al., 2016).

For decades, historical weather data has been utilized by engineers and land planners to calculate the possibilities of future weather events. This historical data gathered through rain gauges, thermometers, and satellites have guided the development of cities across the world. However, recent changes in the earth's climate have caused new challenges, as extreme weather events become more intense and frequent, with trends becoming more difficult to predict (Stanford University, 2020). These weather-related risks could be exacerbated by the fact that many key pieces of the United States' critical infrastructure, such as water and sewage systems, roads, bridges, and power plants, are aging and in need of maintenance or replacement (Intergovernmental Panel on Climate Change, 2012). The U.S Government predicts climate-related changes to continue to damage infrastructure, ecosystems, and social systems that provide essential benefits to communities (Garfin et al., 2019). A review by Stanford University (2020) showed that the actual increase in extreme events was much larger than what had been predicted previously. The authors of this study were able to establish the use of climate prediction models alongside historical observations to create more valid risk assessment tools. However, there remain inaccuracies and unpredictability which must be accounted for.

Communities need to take steps to protect themselves and their property from these events. One of the most effective ways to protect against extreme weather is to be prepared, which can take the form of having emergency supplies, non-perishable food, and access to a safe location. However, with the large effects of climate change, further precautionary measures must be taken to combat the extreme weathers we experience currently and those we expect in the future. The problem is larger than imaginable and therefore measures must be taken on a national level to protect citizens and communities from the effects of extreme weather.

Projections

To ascertain the required protection against extreme weather events, it is important to establish what the current predictions for the future are. According to reports published by the U.S. Government (Garfin et al., 2019), weather events will affect infrastructure, agriculture, health, economy and will disproportionately affect those with lower socioeconomic status.

In terms of infrastructure: transportation systems damage, power outages, fuel shortages, and property damage are all highlighted. Coastal property damage due to high-rising sea levels and coastal erosion is estimated to cost homeowners USD 500 million per year in the U.S. (Jacobo et al., 2022). Waterfront properties are increasingly dealing with flooding, as well as wind and rain damage (Ocean

Home magazine, 2017). Similarly, power and fuel production will be impacted, as increased drought risks affect oil and gas drilling and refining, as well as electricity production since power plants rely on surface water for cooling. Agriculture is also set to face a major decline as a consequence of increases in temperature and possibly changes in water availability, soil erosion, and disease and pest outbreaks. Climate change is predicted to negatively affect health due to rising air and water temperatures that are expected to increase exposure to waterborne and foodborne diseases. Furthermore, the frequency and severity of allergic illnesses as well as the distribution of disease-carrying insects and pests that transmit viruses such as Zika, West Nile, and dengue, are expected to change (Garfin et al., 2019).

Protection Against Flooding

As mentioned above, the risks of flooding in coastal cities around the world are ever-increasing due to alarmingly high sea levels and frequent, destructive rainstorms. Research suggests that by current standards, up to 60 percent of oceanfront communities on the East and Gulf Coasts of the U.S. may experience chronic flooding from climate change by the year 2100 (Dahl et al., 2017). If things worsen, the sea levels could flood major cities including Boston, Newark, Fort Lauderdale, Los Angeles, and New York. As predictions of these cities perishing get closer, plans and solutions for prevention have been discussed for years (Dahl et al., 2017).

In Venice, a historical city in Northern Italy built atop 120 islands and crisscrossed by 177 canals, the risk of vanishing is arguably higher than in any other major city in the world (Phelan, 2022). Harsh estimates show that Venice could be consumed by the sea as early as 2100, with a 4 degrees Celsius temperature increase equating to a sea rise of 5.9ft – enough to flood the city (Zanchettin et al., 2021). In Venice, a solution to protect against rising sea levels has been proposed: the soon-to-be-completed MOSE (Experimental Electromechanical Module) project. The city is planning on installing sea-based defensive barriers made up of 78 mobile gates. Each of these 66ft wide gates is located at strategic points to create a "coastal cordon" to hopefully minimize major flooding events. The barriers lie submerged during periods of calm but rise to block the incoming tide in the lagoon when waters rise to 110cm (3.6ft) (MOSE Venezia, 2022). Although MOSE will be able to combat extreme weather events and extensive flooding of the city, it is unable to stop the chronic impacts of increased water levels within the city (Phelan, 2022).

Similarly, Jakarta, the capital of Indonesia, is facing comparable problems as the city of 11 million residents is battling rising sea levels (Renaldi, 2022). As the city is sinking at approximately 11 inches per year, the Indonesian government has a mega-plan that involves the construction of a 29-mile-long "Giant Sea Wall" (Renaldi, 2022). This sea wall is being developed to obstruct the flow of 13 rivers within Jakarta Bay as well as block storm surges through the development of a 10,000-acre artificial island (Renaldi, 2022). Critics and experts believe this to be a temporary solution, with the construction of a new capital city as an end to the inevitable sinking of their current capital, Jakarta.

Miami, the lively city in South Florida thought to follow in similar footsteps in developing a sea wall after Hurricane Irma left parts of the city underwater. This dramatic $6 Billion proposal was one of the many ideas developed to combat the large effects of climate change (Mazzei, 2021). Other plans included creating surge barriers at the mouth of the Miami River and several other waterways; fortifying sewer plants and fire and police stations to withstand a crush of seawater; elevating or flood-proofing thousands of businesses; and homes as well as planting some mangroves, which can provide the first line of defence against flooding and erosion (Menéndez et al., 2020). Many solutions are being considered and some have been implemented, however, no complete plan has been developed— alarming for a city that may be up to 60% underwater within the next 40 years (Dyer, 2022).

The current reality of climate change and the extreme weather events associated with it are exemplified in these 3 cities as they create multi-billion solutions to problems. However, all solutions seem temporary as the projections of extreme climate change heavily cloud over the future of each of these cities.

Alternative solutions to sea walls have also been developing in recent years. One, nicknamed the 'Dutch-Style Solution' set out by the Delta Project, has been operating in the Netherlands since the late '90s. According to the Watersnood Museum (2022) – a Dutch museum dedicated to all things flooding – it is so effective that the region it protects will only be flooded once every 4,000 years. However, this promising development comes with the caveat – integration takes close to 50 years and costs over USD 7 billion. Other, 'green' alternatives have also been discussed in the literature. These include 'living shorelines,' water-absorbing salt marsh, possibly fortified with sill-like ledges made of rocks, oyster shell bags, or "logs" made of coconut fibres, as well as mangroves (Bennington-Castro, 2017). Salt marshes and mangroves trap sediment and organic matter, allowing them to grow in elevation which affords rising protection against inundation (Bennington-Castro, 2017). According to National Oceanic and Atmospheric Administration (2019), just 15 horizontal feet of marshy terrain can absorb 50 percent of incoming wave energy.

Protection Against Wildfires

Similar to flooding, wildfires are another major extreme weather event caused by climate change. Globally, fire weather seasons have increased by an average of 27% since the 1980s, especially affecting the Amazon, the western forests of North America, and southeast Australia (Boose, 2022). Certain factors contribute to wildfires, including human behaviours, wind levels, vegetation, forest management, and humidity levels. Research shows that climate changes create warmer, drier conditions which alongside increased drought, and a longer fire season are boosting these increases in wildfire risk (National Academies of Sciences Engineering and

Medicine et al., 2017). For much of the U.S. West, projections show that an average annual 1-degree C temperature increase would increase the median burned area per year by as much as 600 percent in some types of forests (National Academies of Sciences Engineering and Medicine et al., 2017). Wildfires can be costly, both in terms of damages and financial expenditures. In 2019, wildfires caused an estimated $4.5 billion in damages in California and Alaska (NICC, 2019). In 2021, California suffered over 9,000 fires which burned over 2.2 million acres and left over 2 million properties at risk (Insurance Information Institute, 2021).

Protection against these costly events begins with the early detection of fires. Currently, civilian reporting and airplane pilots are the main two avenues of spotting wildfires – however – a more proactive approach is needed (Rossi, 2021). One solution proposed by Descartes Lab in California is the use of artificial intelligence, which will be trained to observe satellite images every 10 minutes to identify and interpret thermal infrared data (Wolfe, 2019). This information is further used to deduce whether an active fire is present and consequently report the wildfire to the local authorities (Wolfe, 2019). Testing of this technology has been promising, identifying over 6,000 fires and taking as little as nine minutes to alert authorities. Similarly, a system called ALERTWildfire, which uses tower-mounted cameras, is being trialled in California's Wine Country (ALERTWildfire, 2022). A German company is taking protection straight to consumers by developing low-power sensors that can be hung on trees of properties that can detect carbon monoxide and other gasses (Fialka, 2022).

Another component of protection against wildfires is the prediction of their course – something that is extremely difficult to do since wildfires are erratic by nature. Traditional methods of prediction involved calculating the spread based on the weather, terrain, and dryness of the vegetation (Rossi, 2021). More recently, the use of technology has been developed to aid local and national authorities in forecasting and management of these fires. FireMap, an artificial intelligence tool created by WIFIRElab can make extrapolations using data alongside utility cameras, on-ground sensors, and aircraft with infrared radars (Little, 2022). Tools like this can aid the authorities in identifying where resources should be directed and evacuations should be made.

As the incidence rate of wildfires increases with climate change, early detection and protection against wildfires are two necessary components of combating these events. Another essential component is containing and stopping the fire from further spreading and damaging the environment and infrastructure. Both wet and dry firefighting techniques are currently used (Evans, 2019). The dry method involves creating boundaries around the fire to contain it, often using bulldozers to clear vegetation; whereas the wet methods use fire trucks and large tankers to douse fires – the size depends on the extent of the fire (Evans, 2019). In 2017, California wildfires which affected more than a million acres saw the deployment of a jumbo fire jet carrying 73,000 litres of fire retardant alongside a heavy-lifting helicopter carrying 10,000 litres of water (Fearon, 2020). The use of larger aircraft is the primary method for larger fires, with Canadair firefighting waterbombers being the gold standard (Last, 2022). These amphibious planes, first created in the 1960s, can scoop large volumes of water (up to 6,000L) from lakes and rivers and drop a mix of water and fire suppressant over the fire (Last, 2022). As France faced the 'fire of the century' earlier this year, the shortage of these planes due to low production and aging fleets was highlighted (Last, 2022). This resulted in companies like AirBus stepping in to convert their planes into firefighting planes which will be able to carry three times the amount of water as the Canadair aircraft.

Protection Against Extreme Heat

Climate change has increased the frequency of extreme weather events globally. In 2022, dozens of countries reached their hottest temperatures recorded, with the United Kingdom recording 40 degrees Celsius. In 2021, Lytton BC broke the Canadian heat record with recorded temperatures of over 49.6 degrees Celsius

(BBC, 2022). Extreme heat is affecting the globe more than ever. Heat waves have become a regular and hazardous occurrence due to climate change, affecting temperature regulation in cities as well as exposing citizens to heat-related illnesses (CDC, 2022). In the US, heat kills more people per year than any other weather event (Bendix & Associated Press, 2022). The Global Burden of Diseases, Injuries, and Risk Factors Study indicated that extreme heat and cold exposure can increase or decrease the risk of mortality for a diverse set of causes of death (Burkart et al., 2021). Globally, the authors estimated 356,000 deaths related to heat in 2019 which highlights the relevance of temperature as a risk factor for human health (Burkart et al., 2021).

Heatwaves are a dangerous reality due to increasingly warmer temperatures caused by climate change which have brought along an array of issues. Heatwaves can cause health problems, destruction of crops, and put an additional strain on electricity networks (Fischer et al., 2020). In urban areas, further issues are caused by the "heat island effect," in which the city's asphalt and buildings absorb and release heat (H&V Content Team).

Reducing the impacts of heatwaves can be done through a combination of short-term solutions, such as creating supportive infrastructure, adequate cooling systems, and access to medical help — and long-term solutions such as mitigation of greenhouse gases and adopting renewable energies (Ramesh et al., 2018). Cities are increasingly attempting to plan in ways that address this issue. For example, Tokyo is adopting planning approaches to increase public green spaces to help reduce temperature (Hamano and Sonobe). In a report by the Chief Public Health Officer of Canada, increasing urban green space to reduce outdoor temperatures, as well as increasing vegetation to provide more tree canopy, are two viable options suggested to proactively design for heat in urban areas (May 2017). The best example of a design to protect against extreme heat is that of Singapore. Since 1967, Singapore has embarked on its 'garden city' initiative which has led to over 100 hectares of skyrise greenery which included vertical planting and roof gardens that can help temperatures drop by 2-3 degrees (Oldfield, 2018). Across the US, further steps are being taken to reduce the impact of increased heat: New York City has seen more than 500,000m² of roof space covered in a white reflective coating which is 23 degrees cooler than a black roof (Oldfield, 2018). Los Angeles on the other hand has applied a white-coloured sealant onto roads which supposedly can reduce the temperature by up to 5.5 degrees Celsius (Broom, 2019). Other protective solutions include the use of water for cooling and reducing the effects of heat. Across the world, major cities have implemented water misters in urban areas to provide temporary moments of relief for pedestrians. Ideas of contemporary heat-proof cities that would use ponds, pools, fountains, sprinklers, and misting systems to cool outdoor spaces are another promising alternative (Fleming, 2020). A study by the University of South Wales showed that adding water features and cool coatings would reduce cooling requirements by 29–43%, with temperature samples taken adjacent to such water features showing up to 10 degrees Celsius lower temperatures (Oldfield, 2018).

According to the World Health Organization (2022), climate change has made drier regions drier as the heat increases evaporation. This has led to increased droughts in dry, warm areas such as the United Arab Emirates which in 2021 suffered the longest recorded meteorological droughts in the past two decades (Zaman, 2021). In response to these bouts of water scarcity, scientists in this region have developed drone technology that can induce rain by emitting an electric charge inside clouds (Kissel, 2021). This new form of weather manipulation known as "cloud seeding" offers hope across the world to regions facing similar issues. Although the long-term effects of this chemical intervention on agriculture and ecology are unknown, innovation to this degree is the future to protect against extreme weather and climate change (Hawksley, 2021).

Conclusion

The impact of climate change and the consequential increase in extreme temperatures can no longer be denied. Research shows the inevitable changes in our climate and projections show a fast-approaching reality that requires thoughtful planning. Necessary steps must be taken to identify sources of future issues and mitigate them to protect ourselves against extreme weather conditions. Areas that are at risk for extreme climate-related damage have already begun to implement solutions to combat extreme weather conditions such as flooding, wildfires, and extreme heat. Projections and predictions of the severity of impact are useful in preparing the solutions for protections which can be both short- and long-term solutions. Technology is increasingly being adopted in protection against extreme weather, which shows a trajectory in the right direction, especially as predictions of future climate events are alarming. This use of technology allows novel solutions to unforeseen weather events that are a consequence of climate change and gives us a fighting chance to protect ourselves and our infrastructure.

References

BBC. (2022, Autumn 7). As the Earth heats up, high-temperature records are being broken more often. CBC News. Retrieved from https://www.cbc.ca/news/world/weather-records-1.6523930

Bell, J. E., Herring, S. C., Jantarasami, L., Adrianopoli, C., Benedict, K., Conlon, K., Escobar, V., Hess, J., Luvall, J., Garcia-Pando, C. P., Quattrochi, D., Runkle, J., & Schreck, C. J., III. (2016). Ch. 4: Impacts of extreme events on Human Health. The Impacts of Climate Change on Human Health in the United States: A Scientific Assessment, 99–128. Retrieved from https://health2016.globalchange.gov/extreme-events

Bendix, A., & Associated Press. (2022, July 20). How extreme heat becomes deadly — and how to protect yourself and your pets. NBC News. Retrieved from https://www.nbcnews.com/health/health-news/extreme-heat-deadly-how-to-stay-safe-rcna38916

Bennington-Castro, J. (2017, July 27). Walls won't save our cities from rising seas. Here's what will. NBC News. Retrieved from https://www.nbcnews.com/mach/science/walls-won-t-save-our-cities-rising-seas-here-s-ncna786811

Boose, Y. (2022, August 18). Are wildfires getting worse due to climate change? Blog. Retrieved from https://blog.breezometer.com/are-wildfires-becoming-more-common/

Broom, D. (2019, August 30). How LA plans to be 1.6°C cooler by 2050. World Economic Forum. Retrieved from https://www.weforum.org/agenda/2019/08/los-angeles_climate-change_urban-heat_reflective-asphalt

Burkart, K. G., Brauer, M., Aravkin, A. Y., Godwin, W. W., Hay, S. I., He, J., Iannucci, V. C., Larson, S. L., Lim, S. S., Liu, J., Murray, C. J. L., Zheng, P., Zhou, M., & Stanaway, J. D. (2021). Estimating the cause-specific relative risks of non-optimal temperature on daily mortality: a two-part modelling approach applied to the Global Burden of Disease Study. Lancet, 398(10301), 685–697. doi: 10.1016/S0140-6736(21)01700-1

Dahl, K. A., Spanger-Siegfried, E., Caldas, A., & Udvardy, S. (2017). Effective inundation of continental United States communities with 21st-century sea level rise. Elementa (Washington, D.C.), 5(0), 37. doi: 10.1525/elementa.234

Delta plan – watersnoodmuseum. (2022). Watersnoodmuseum. Nl. Retrieved from https://watersnoodmuseum.nl/en/knowledgecentre/delta-plan/

Dyer, A. (2022, September 15). Scientists warn South Florida coastal cities will be affected by sea level rise. CBS Miami. Retrieved from https://www.cbsnews.com/miami/news/scientists-warn-south-florida-coastal-cities-will-be-affected-by-sea-level-rise/

Evans, G. (2019, November 17). How do you fight extreme wildfires? BBC. Retrieved from https://www.bbc.com/news/world-50410481

Excell, J. (2018, February). Wildfire warriors: the latest developments in aerial firefighting technology. The Engineer. Retrieved from https://www.theengineer.co.uk/content/in-depth/wildfire-warriors-the-latest-developments-in-aerial-firefighting-technology

Fearon, R. (2020). Wildfire technology: Tackling the spread of wilderness fires with digital tech. Discovery. Retrieved from https://www.discovery.com/technology/wildlife-technology

Fialka, J. (2022, May 5). Wildfires on the rise, but new tech could help in the fight. E&E News. Retrieved from https://www.eenews.net/articles/wildfires-on-the-rise-but-new-tech-could-help-in-the-fight/

Fleming, S. (2020, August 17). This is how European cities are fighting back against heat waves. World Economic Forum. Retrieved from https://www.weforum.org/agenda/2020/08/europe-fights-back-against-heatwaves/

Garfin, G., Gonzalez, P., Breshears, D., Brooks, K., Brown, H., Elias, E., Gunasekara, A., Huntly, N., Maldonado, J., Mantua, N., Margolis, H., McAfee, S., Middleton, B., & Udall, B. (2019). The fourth national climate assessment, chapter 25: Southwest. In Earth and Space Science Open Archive (pp. 1–470). doi: 10.1002/essoar.10500376.1

Hawksley, R. (2021, July 22). Dubai's fake rain offers hope that we can innovate our way out of the climate crisis. Independent. Retrieved from https://www.independent.co.uk/climate-change/opinion/dubai-fake-rain-climate-crisis-b1888450.html

Insurance Information Institute. (2021). Facts + statistics: Wildfires. Iii.org. Retrieved from https://www.iii.org/fact-statistic/facts-statistics-wildfires

Intergovernmental Panel on Climate Change. (2012). Managing the risks of extreme events and disasters to advance climate change adaptation: Special report of the intergovernmental panel on climate change (C. B. Field, V. Barros, T. F. Stocker, & Q. Dahe, Eds.). Cambridge University Press.

Islands of Venice: Detailed information and Overview, list of area and inhabitants, and a travel guide of all inhabited islands in Venice. (n.d.). Venice-Guide.Info. Retrieved from http://www.venice-guide.info/Islands_Venice.php

Jacobo, J., Manzo, D., & Zee, G. (2022, November 7). How climate change and rising sea levels are transforming coastlines around the world. ABC News. Retrieved from https://abcnews.go.com/US/climate-change-rising-sea-levels-transforming-coastlines-world/story?id=91681973

Kissel, T. (2021). Greekreporter.com. Retrieved from https://greekreporter.com/2021/07/22/rain-drones-new-technology-uae-dubai/#:~:text=Scientists%20in%20the%20United%20Arab,reach%20above%2040%20degrees%20Celsius.

Last, J. (2022, August). How an aging fleet of Canadairs is keeping Europe's wildfires at bay. CBC News. Retrieved from https://www.cbc.ca/news/world/canadair-water-bomber-wildfire-europe-1.6553592

Little, J. (2022, September 17). UC San Diego creates software to help fight wildfires around California. NBC San Diego. Retrieved from https://www.nbcsandiego.com/news/local/uc-san-diego-creates-software-to-help-fight-fires-around-california/3048962/

May, T. (2017). Reducing urban heat islands to protect health in Canada. Canada.Ca. Retrieved from https://www.canada.ca/en/services/health/publications/healthy-living/reducing-urban-heat-islands-protect-health-canada.html

Mazzei, P. (2021, June 2). A 20-foot sea wall? Miami faces the hard choices of climate change. The New York Times. https://www.nytimes.com/2021/06/02/us/miami-fl-seawall-hurricanes.html

Menéndez, P., Losada, I. J., Torres-Ortega, S., Narayan, S., & Beck, M. W. (2020). The global flood protection benefits of mangroves. Scientific Reports, 10(1), 4404. doi: 10.1038/s41598-020-61136-

MOSE Venezia. (2022). Mosevenezia.Eu. Retrieved from https://www.mosevenezia.eu/project/?lang=en

National Academies of Sciences Engineering and Medicine, Division on Earth and Life Studies, & Board on Atmospheric Sciences & Climate. (2017). Review of the draft climate science special report. National Academies Press.

NCEI. (2022). Billion-dollar weather and climate disasters. Noaa.gov. Retrieved from https://www.ncei.noaa.gov/access/billions/events/US/2000-2017

NICC. (2019). Wildland Fire Summary and Statistics Annual Report 2019. Nifc.gov. Retrieved from https://www.predictiveservices.nifc.gov/intelligence/2019_statssumm/intro_summary19.pdf

Ocean Home magazine. (2017, June 22). The environmental factors that can affect a home by the sea. Ocean Home Magazine. Retrieved from https://www.oceanhomemag.com/outdoor-living/the-environmental-factors-that-can-affect-a-home-by-the-sea/

Oldfield, P. (2018, August 15). What would a heat-proof city look like? The Guardian. Retrieved from https://www.theguardian.com/cities/2018/aug/15/what-heat-proof-city-look-like

Phelan, J. (2022, September). Italy's plan to save Venice from sinking. BBC. Retrieved from https://www.bbc.com/future/article/20220927-italys-plan-to-save-venice-from-sinking

Renaldi, A. (2022, July 29). Indonesia's giant capital city is sinking. Can the government's plan save it? National Geographic. Retrieved from https://www.nationalgeographic.com/environment/article/indonesias-giant-capital-city-is-sinking-can-the-governments-plan-save-it

Rossi, M. (2021, August 20). From supercomputers to fire-starting drones, these tools help fight wildfires. Smithsonian Magazine. Retrieved from https://www.smithsonianmag.com/innovation/from-supercomputers-to-fire-starting-drones-these-tools-help-fight-wildfires-180978421/

Stanford University. (2020, March 18). Climate change means more extreme weather than predicted. Stanford News. Retrieved from https://news.stanford.edu/2020/03/18/climate-change-means-extreme-weather-predicted/

The Lancet. (2021). Health in a world of extreme heat. Lancet, 398(10301), 641. doi: 10.1016/S0140-6736(21)01860-2

United Nations. (2022). What is climate change? | United Nations. Retrieved from https://www.un.org/en/climatechange/what-is-climate-change

US Department of Commerce, & National Oceanic. (2019). What is a living shoreline? Retrieved from https://oceanservice.noaa.gov/facts/living-shoreline.htm

WHO. (2022). Drought. Who.int. Retrieved from https://www.who.int/health-topics/drought

Wildfire, A. (2022). ALERT wildfire. Alertwildfire.org. Retrieved from https://www.alertwildfire.org/about/

Wolfe, A. (2019, December 19). A look at how Descartes Labs is leveraging AI to alert fire managers of wildfires and decrease the damage to homes and habitats across the US. *Business Insider.* Retrieved from https://www.businessinsider.com/how-descartes-labs-leveraging-artificial-intelligence-fight-wildfires-2019-12

Zaman, S. (2021, January 26). Arabian Gulf experiencing the longest recorded meteorological drought over last two decades. *Gulf News.* Retrieved from https://gulfnews.com/uae/arabian-gulf-experiencing-longest-recorded-meteorological-drought-over-last-two-decades-1.76727771

Zanchettin, D., Bruni, S., Raicich, F., Lionello, P., Adloff, F., Androsov, A., Antonioli, F., Artale, V., Carminati, E., Ferrarin, C., Fofonova, V., Nicholls, R. J., Rubinetti, S., Rubino, A., Sannino, G., Spada, G., Thiéblemont, R., Tsimplis, M., Umgiesser, G., ... Zerbini, S. (2021). Sea-level rise in Venice: historic and future trends (review article). *Natural Hazards and Earth System Sciences, 21*(8), 2643–2678. doi: 10.5194/nhess-21-2643-2021

Chapter 10
Workforce Developments

Razan Ahmed

Introduction

Climate change is causing issues in society that we have never seen before, from excessive heat to flooding caused by sea level rise. It is compelling us not just to construct adaptations for a changing planet but also to undertake the massive challenge of creating green infrastructure and shifting from carbon-emitting fossil fuels to renewable energy. And each component of the climate conundrum will necessitate more participation from individuals from all areas of life. Policy directions aimed at achieving a just transition should assist employees in transitioning away from industries vulnerable to disruption and into other jobs.

Labour Market

Regulations and regulatory frameworks connected to climate change will cause changes in the industry (supply side) and consumer habits (demand side). This suggests a significant shift in general economic activity, mostly affecting businesses and workers, either directly or indirectly. As a result, labour market institutions will need to cope with these developments early on to reduce the possible negative consequences and capture new possibilities (Miranda, 2010).

Regulations aimed at the supply and demand channels will affect labour markets by focusing consumer demand for cleaner products (goods and services) and dragging the production system in the same direction (Miranda, 2010). In general, the goal of these restrictions is to gradually diminish demand for items that are or are considered to be environmentally destructive in their end use or method of manufacture while increasing demand for energy efficiency and non-polluting products. Indeed, climate change has already begun to alter consumer preferences and behaviours, mostly through increasing social awareness and social conscience, which leads to a desire for greener options.

Climate change regulations that indirectly impact labour markets (Miranda, 2010):

Czech Republic: Biofuel Blending Requirements: The Czech government mandates minimum biofuel blending levels for gasoline and diesel used in transportation. Companies that distribute petrol and diesel transportation fuels on the market are required to add a minimum quantity of biofuels.

France: Sustainable Energy Provisions: The 2009 Finance Law includes provisions to improve finance for energy efficiency expenditures and renewable energy, such as zero-interest financing for energy-efficient dwelling purchases and 100% loans for energy-efficient refurbishment.

Germany: Special Fund for Energy Efficiency in Small and Medium-Sized Enterprises: The fund was formed by the Federal Ministry of Economics and the KfW bank to assist SMEs in overcoming knowledge and economic obstacles to implementing energy-efficient solutions. The program is divided into incentives for SMEs to engage energy efficiency consultants and low-interest loans for investment in energy-saving measures.

Climate change regulations that directly impact labour markets (Miranda, 2010):

United States: Green Jobs Act (2007): The Green Jobs Act provides competitive funds from the Federal Government to organizations to carry out training to create energy efficiency and renewable energy sectors workforce.

Australia: National Green Jobs Corps: Federal funding has been committed to providing 26 weeks of green job training and practical experience to long-term jobless kids. Tasks include bush regeneration and the cultivation of native trees, the conservation of animal and fish habitats, the construction/ restoration of walking and nature trails, and training and hands-on practice in the construction of energy-efficient architectural elements.

Spain: Automotive Sector Competitiveness Plan: The plan provides funding for a wide variety of initiatives targeted at boosting the auto industry's competitiveness through improvements in the energy efficiency of manufacturing processes, goods, and services. It provides enterprises with the opportunity to access grants and loans to increase the technical capabilities of their personnel.

Greener policies appear to be accepted and adopted by consumers in their behaviour. According to a Eurobarometer study, 50% of EU residents support charging items with big environmental footprints, and 83% of respondents said they consider the environmental effect of products before purchasing them (Docquiert, 2009). These market-driven laws are projected to cause the expansion and contraction of specific economic sectors and industries, affecting labour markets. Green labelling activities may necessitate new green analytical skills and standards, and more employment opportunities may be generated as a result. Other operations, such as procurement requirements and legal processes, would also grow (Miranda, 2010).

Until recently, quantitative analyses of the effects of climate change policy on employment were limited. The information supplied is largely about individual economic sectors rather than labour markets in general. However, the work done in this regard tends to suggest that, notwithstanding the dangers involved, the economic restructuring caused by climate change regulation provides the opportunity to generate a little positive net employment increase (Miranda, 2010).

EGS manufacturing is often more labour-demanding than traditional industries. According to the International Energy Agency (2009), the high labour intensity of the EGS industry -

notably the renewable energy sector - is explained in part by the fact that renewable energy sources are still not cost-effective (Miranda, 2010). This indicates that for a given quantity of output, these activities necessitate more inputs. As a result, the IEA projects that for every billion dollars spent on sustainable energy technologies, 30 000 new positions will be created (Miranda, 2010).

According to additional research, the renewable energy sector creates more employment than the fossil fuel-based energy sector per unit of energy provided (Wei, Patadia, & Kammen, 2010). While the bulk of renewable energy activities, such as energy efficiency, smart metering, and renewable energy generation, have a greater labour intensity, some activities, such as carbon capture and storage (CCS), have a significantly lower labour intensity due to their capital intensity (IEA, 2009). However, the requirement for R&D of CCS technology means that research positions in this area may rise significantly to fulfill the demands of pilot programs. Europe has 66 CCS projects, accounting for 25% of the worldwide total (Global CCS Institute, 2009).

The aggregate net job growth forecasts present a very hopeful picture of the changes that labour markets will face in the coming years. However, the changes that will occur in labour markets will result in both winners and losers. Understanding the dynamics of these changes will be critical for policymakers attempting to maximize the advantages and minimize the dangers of the low-carbon economic transition (Miranda, 2010).

The United Nations Environment Programme (UNEP) anticipates that when climate change regulations are implemented, and the economy is directed toward higher sustainability, labour markets will be impacted in at least four ways (UNEP, ILO, ITUC, IOE, 2008a). For starters, more employment will be generated in some circumstances, such as when pollution-control systems are added to existing industrial equipment. Second, some jobs will be substituted, such as when switching "from fossil fuels to renewable energy sources, or from truck manufacturing to rail car manufacturing, or from landfilling and waste incineration to recycling." Thirdly, certain employees may be lost without a direct replacement, such as when packaging materials are discouraged or forbidden and production ceases (Miranda, 2010). Fourth, many existing jobs (especially those of plumbers, electricians, metal workers, and labourers) will be altered and redefined as day-to-day skill sets, work techniques, and profiles are greened (UNEP, ILO, ITUC, IOE, 2008a p. 3).

In the short run, employment in directly impacted sectors will be destroyed, but new ones will be created in replacement industries. Jobs will be lost in carbon-intensive industries, developing slowly or even declining. New employment is predicted to be produced in low-carbon industries, which are often more labour-intensive than traditional industries (e.g. renewable energy vs. conventional energy). However, as low-carbon technologies become more competitive and established, the predicted net employment creation is likely to decline. As a result, such job improvements cannot be sustained over a 10–15-year period (Miranda, 2010).

Climate change policies will have an influence on the economy in the medium term, generating and destroying employment as behaviour changes and value chains alter. The impact on employment will be heavily influenced by outside factors such as raw material prices (gas, oil, etc.) that determine the price gap between low-carbon innovations and traditional remedies, as well as regulatory policies that encourage businesses to implement more energy-efficient production techniques (Miranda, 2010). Rises in typical energy prices, along with carbon pricing laws, will boost the competitiveness of renewable energy technology, resulting in job development in this industry.

Long-term innovation and the development of new technologies will open up new avenues for investment and growth. It is envisaged that employment would be produced in low-carbon technology research and development. The findings will spur more investment and employment growth in these industries (Miranda, 2010). This virtuous cycle exemplifies the beneficial effects that innovation and technological development may have on economic growth and restructuring. However, as the green economy expands, there will be greater demand for highly trained and certified labour capable of meeting the expanding technology and innovative demands.

Canada

While Canadian scholars and politicians excel at considering the environmental and economic implications of transition, we pay far less attention to workforce development. The shift to a zero-carbon economy will significantly impact the Canadian economy and labour market. Some businesses will shrink, while others will adapt, and green industries will develop dramatically. While the effects will be felt throughout the country, towns that rely on carbon-intensive sectors for employment will be struck the hardest. According to most forecasts, the transition to net zero will produce more employment than it displaces, but those jobs may not be in the same communities (Harding & Myers, 2022). Even if they are, they may necessitate distinct abilities. The transition to a less carbon-intensive economy would influence the skills required for up to one-quarter of all occupations. The shift to a net-zero climate policy will have far-reaching consequences. The federal government has finished a nationwide consultation process to determine how its future "Just Transition" legislation would aid in the transition to a lower-carbon economy while fulfilling environmental goals, preserving economic development, and including workers and their communities (Harding & Myers, 2022).

Workforce development is a critical component of the problem. Policy directions aimed at achieving a just transition should assist employees in transitioning away from industries vulnerable to disruption and into other jobs. While Canadian scholars and politicians excel at considering the environmental and economic implications of transition, we pay far less attention to workforce development (Harding & Myers, 2022). The federal government should rely on its experience with worker displacement from Canada's recent shift away from coal. Indeed, the auditor general concluded that there was an overreliance on existing supports and services, with insufficient new ones tailored expressly to serve coal miners and their communities (Harding & Myers, 2022). Furthermore, the federal government failed to monitor or report on the equitable transition for coal employees, and it functioned without a clear framework.

If Canada wants to make the possibilities created by the transition to net zero available to people who will be most affected, it must adopt a more strategic, evidence-based, and place-based approach to workforce development and learn from its past failures (Harding & Myers, 2022). The transition to net zero will have the greatest impact on natural resource occupations, notably in the oil and gas sector, which has distinct employment geographies. According to analyses conducted by the Canadian Climate Institute and the Canadian Centre for Policy Alternatives (CCPA), oil and gas jobs are mostly concentrated in small and medium-sized towns, with many located in rural areas with little economic diversification (Harding & Myers, 2022). The exact number of jobs lost may be minimal, but their absence will be felt deeply in those communities. In the United States, six million industrial jobs were lost between 1990 and 2007, primarily in smaller "rust belt" areas with minimal economic diversification. Following then, job growth happened in other industries (mainly in services) in other areas (predominantly coastal states) (Harding & Myers, 2022). The majority of the displaced workers did not relocate to find a job. Instead, many stayed in their hometowns, where they frequently struggled to find a job. Their towns became "pockets of hardship," with high rates of long-term unemployment and political disenchantment (Harding & Myers, 2022).

Canada's approach to fair transitions policy should take a place-based strategy, which develops jobs in places where jobs are lost and offers assistance to ensure people can do them. Economic growth is critical. The continuation of unemployment and pay inequality in the United States over the last two decades has sparked demands for a revitalization of place-based economic development initiatives

(Harding & Myers, 2022). This is supported by current Canadian research on fair transition, which advocates for regional economic growth plans that capitalize on local assets. Economic development creates jobs, while workforce development assists local employees in transitioning into such occupations. (Harding & Myers, 2022) It helps them through an increasingly complicated labour market and prepares them for these new tasks.

Strategies

The present increase in commodity prices affords chances to examine new and creative methods of workforce development that are emerging in Canada (Harding & Myers, 2022). Several action areas assist us in narrowing down what a better response for employees would look like. Workers will require new abilities to execute new tasks and assistance navigating an increasingly complicated labour market.

Improve the quality and accessibility of career counselling: Utilize extensive study on professional development, its problems, and strategies to improve, as well as investigate financing sources, such as the Canada training benefit for career assistance (Harding & Myers, 2022).

Concentrate on sectoral models that offer career counselling and/ or skill training: The emphasis might be on the disrupted industry, such as the Estevan Coal Transition Centre, which provides support to displaced coal workers. It might potentially aim for rapid local or regional expansion (Harding & Myers, 2022). EDGE UP, an ongoing Future Abilities Centre-funded project, does both by assisting managers displaced from the oil and gas industry in expanding their current skills to enter Calgary's developing IT business.

Workers are frequently unaware of the available support services or do not use them.

Examine hub models: Hubs offer a variety of services and assistance in a single place or network of sites, with focused marketing and branding. Hubs might also provide services to local firms, such as staff upskilling and business services (Harding & Myers, 2022).

Supporters must avoid replicating the massive female pay disparity in fossil fuel industries.

Broad qualifying criteria: Efforts to assist employees in transition must not be limited to individuals who have been immediately displaced, who are often Canadian-born men earning nearly double the national average. Rather, they must incorporate the whole local workforce, particularly support workers in businesses like food and lodging, who are more likely to be female, racialized, and underpaid (Harding & Myers, 2022). Individual qualities should not be used to establish eligibility.

Organizations that provide services and support will need to make continuous improvements to their programs.

Implement design thinking, quick learning, and improvement cycles: To guarantee that policies and programs suit the requirements and preferences of the target audiences, program design should include user-centered design. At its core should be a data-driven approach to learning and continuous improvement based on a test-learn-adapt strategy. With each consecutive cohort, it should strive towards greater quality and efficacy (Harding & Myers, 2022).

Several studies have found that compensation and benefits in the fast-rising renewable energy business are lower than in the traditional construction and energy industries. Unionized workers in these more traditional industries have battled hard to win robust pay, benefit, and safety standards ("High-Road Workforce Guide for City Climate Action," 2021). Such safeguards are sometimes lacking in new sectors. Cities must promote rules and regulations that safeguard workers and arrange public investments to encourage good firms to guarantee that the renewable energy transition does not undermine local labour standards and produce unstable, low-paying employment.

The secret to success will differ depending on the city. It will be determined by political will, partnerships with community partners, relationships between local government departments, financial resources, personnel availability, and other considerations. For example, if there are many training providers and programs but the trained employees are having difficulty finding excellent employment, city initiatives to increase demand for skilled people will be more beneficial than launching another training program. In contrast, if there is a lot of clean energy and other construction activity but there aren't enough trained employees or disadvantaged workers engaging, a training-side intervention like a pre-apprenticeship program might be very beneficial ("High-Road Workforce Guide for City Climate Action," 2021). Maybe there are enough training programs and the demand for workers is great, but the programs and potential employers are not efficiently connected. In this situation, a city's greatest function may be as a connection between training providers and companies, requesting employer opinion on the skills they require or assisting in the creation of pipelines to employment for training graduates.

There is a demand-and-supply dynamic in all connections in the local labour ecosystem. An apprenticeship program, for example, can stimulate demand for graduates of a community-based apprenticeship-readiness training program while also supplying qualified and trained employees to local firms. Solidifying these supply-and-demand linkages may benefit employees, companies, and the community as a whole ("High-Road Workforce Guide for City Climate Action," 2021).

Implementing a high-road workforce strategy as part of a city's climate initiatives necessitates thoughtful policy and program design to ensure employment quality as well as fair job access. Some climate-related activities, such as utility-scale renewables installation, transportation infrastructure, or extensive energy retrofits of major commercial buildings, need highly specialized and qualified employees. Higher salaries and greater benefits are often necessary to recruit and maintain a talented staff. There may be a prevailing wage norm in public works construction, providing greater compensation that attracts employees with stronger expertise ("High-Road Workforce Guide for City Climate Action," 2021). Even outside of government contracts, big or aggregated small initiatives can generate the economies of scale required to impose more severe contractual terms. In contrast, skills, training, and safety requirements are generally weaker or not enforced on a smaller scale and less centralized or disaggregated work, such as home retrofits or rooftop solar. Under these conditions, worker compensation tends to be lower, retaining qualified staff is difficult, and career growth opportunities are limited.

Low employment quality, as well as hurdles to entry and progression, can have political repercussions for community support for climate-change mitigation efforts. Unionized workers in the high-skill, high-quality utility sector may be concerned that dispersed rooftop solar installation may erode labour standards across the business ("High-Road Workforce Guide for City Climate Action," 2021). Underrepresented or disadvantaged persons may not envision a future in a low-carbon economy until mechanisms to promote career-track employment access are implemented. Green jobs training programs may come to be viewed as just another low-wage, dead-end option that fails to provide upward mobility by community organizations campaigning for employment for jobless city people.

Fortunately, city employees have several options to increase both employment quality and equal access in the current context. Cities should use their contracting and procurement processes to guarantee that construction contractors give disadvantaged municipal employees access to high-quality jobs. They can collaborate with utilities to develop efficiency rebate programs that rely on contractors with a track record of providing high-quality work and excellent jobs ("High-Road Workforce Guide for City

Climate Action," 2021). They can collaborate with local and state authorities to create demand for climate employment through low-income solar installation initiatives that give on-the-job training for those in specific training programs. They may sponsor renewable energy and building training initiatives to help city workers start a career ("High-Road Workforce Guide for City Climate Action," 2021).

Conclusion

Community investments, financial support for employees and municipalities, and programs for local economic growth should be part of the response to workers displaced by net-zero climate change. Workforce development is vital, and we will need to go beyond current ways. Lessons must be drawn from the coal sector transition to ensure that the response fulfills the requirements of employees and their communities. Identifying the correct employment models is a difficult undertaking that involves community buy-in as well as government, business, and service providers.

References

Docquiert, J. (2009, July 31). 45% des Français favorables à une taxe carbone. Retrieved from https://www.lesechos.fr/2009/07/environnement-45-des-francais-favorables-a-une-taxe-carbone-461219

Ensuring Green Growth in a Time of Crisis; The Role of Energy Technology. (2009). IEA. Retrieved from www.iea.org/Papers/2009/ensuring_green_growth.pdf

Global CCS Institute. (2009). Strategic Analysis of the Global Status of Carbon Capture and Storage, Report 1: Status of Carbon Capture and Storage Projects Globally. Retrieved from https://www.globalccsinstitute.com/archive/hub/publications/5751/report-1-status-carbon-capture-and-storage-projects-globally.pdf

Harding & Myers. (2022, October 5). Workforce development is the missing piece in the transition to net zero. Retrieved from https://policyoptions.irpp.org/magazines/september-2022/coal-labour-transition/

High-Road Workforce Guide for City Climate Action. (2021). Inclusive Economics. Retrieved from https://www.usdn.org/uploads/cms/documents/workforce-guide_4.12.21_form.pdf

Miranda, C. M. H. (2010, July 1). Greening Jobs and Skills. Retrieved from https://www.oecd-ilibrary.org/docserver/5kmbjgl8sd0r-en.pdf?expires=1672460816

UNEP, ILO, IOE, ITUC. (2008, September). Green Jobs: Towards Decent Work in a Sustainable, Low-Carbon World (Full report). Retrieved from https://www.ilo.org/global/topics/green-jobs/publications/WCMS_158727/lang--en/index.htm

Wei, M., Patadia, S., & Kammen, D. M. (2010). Putting renewables and energy efficiency to work: How many jobs can the clean energy industry generate in the US? Energy Policy, 38(2), 919–931. doi: 10.1016/j.enpol.2009.10.044

Conclusion

This book has covered topics encapsulating the themes of food security, energy production, and livelihood changes. Despite the expanse of topics considered, this book is by no means an exhaustive review of adaptations to climate change. Instead, this book intended to provide a precursory introduction to the topic and recent developments.

We hope that readers can gain optimism and encouragement in furthering attempts to challenge seemingly inevitable mass extinctions in the near future. Indeed, this book is a precursor; an introduction to the conversations, potential solutions, and concerns arising from the transition to renewable energy and other methods of adaptation to climate change.